LETTER **BOMB**

PARALLAX  Re-visions of Culture and Society

Stephen G. Nichols, Gerald Prince, and Wendy Steiner

SERIES EDITORS

LETTER

Nuclear Holocaust and the Exploding Word

BOMB

PETER SCHWENGER

The Johns Hopkins University Press   Baltimore and London

The Johns Hopkins University Press
701 West 40th Street, Baltimore, Maryland 21211-2190
The Johns Hopkins Press Ltd., London

Library of Congress Cataloging-in-Publication Data

Schwenger, Peter, 1942–
    Letter bomb : nuclear holocaust and the exploding word / Peter
Schwenger
        p.   cm. — (Parallax)
    Includes bibliographical references and index.
    ISBN 0-8018-4487-8 (hc). — ISBN 0-8018-4488-6 (paper)
    1. Deconstruction. 2. Nuclear warfare and literature. I. Title.
II. Series: Parallax (Baltimore, Md.)
PN98.D43S39   1992
801'.95—dc20   92-18277

A catalog record for this book is available from the British Library

Chapter 1, "Post Nuclear Post Card," has been published in *Papers on Language & Literature* 26.1 (1990): 164–81; chapter 2, "Circling Ground Zero," has been published in *PMLA* 106.2 (1991): 251–61. Copyright © 1990 by the Board of Trustees, Southern Illinois University. Reprinted by permission. Brief portions of this work have been excerpted from "Writing the Unthinkable," *Critical Inquiry* 13 (1986): 33–48.

For Steven Bruhm

Contents

Acknowledgments

Parts of this book have been read in manuscript by Maggie Berg, Heinz and Eva Bruhl, Ross Chambers, H. Bruce Franklin, Tom Gerry, Sandy Petry, Eugene Vance and, repeatedly, Steven Bruhm. I wish to thank all these people for their time and their insights.

Ronald Foley Macdonald, of the National Film Board of Canada, provided invaluable material on Tarkovsky; David Huisman introduced me to the Green Man.

I've been fortunate in my editors. Eric Wirth and Claire Cooke edited "Circling Ground Zero" for *PMLA,* and I learned much from them. Roberta Hughey then edited the entire manuscript with acuity and elegance. For their professionalism and efficiency I thank Eric Halpern and all those at Johns Hopkins University Press who were involved in the production of this book.

Initiator

This book was initiated, as is often the case, by another book. One autumn day in 1983, a student of mine gave me a copy of Raymond Briggs's nuclear parable, *When the Wind Blows,* which I riffled through quickly while eating lunch in my office, then went on to a busy afternoon. The day finally calmed down, but I did not; there was an intense anxiety in me that I could not account for, assigning it first to one cause and then to another. Nothing fit. Only a long walk allowed me to realize that a book so innocuous as to be first cousin to a comic book had invaded my unconscious and was still working there. How could this be? How could a book do this to me when I so plainly didn't want it done? But this, it then struck me, was a question for a literary critic: it became my question for the next seven years. Along the way the question shifted. It began as a study of literature about nuclear holocaust—that is, a study of what literature could "tell" us about nuclear holocaust and our reactions to its suspended potential. The nature of the telling itself was always, of course, in the foreground—but so complicated was this nature where the nuclear referent was concerned that the question soon generated another, its reversed mirror image: the book became a study of what the nuclear referent could tell us about literature.

The changes in this book, and in its author, took place within a larger context of change—political, psychological, and artistic. In the autumn of 1983, for example, the magazines had been full of the upcoming television special *The Day After,* whose nuclear subject was unprecedented. As it turned out, there were only too many precedents, most of them taken from the stock format of the Hollywood catastrophe movie. But the mere anticipation of seeing images of what we had for so long been unwilling or unable to see—this anticipation was itself a kind of inner vision, releasing images and emotions that had been denied or repressed. And before Briggs published his book of black humor, literature had already begun (with, for example, *Riddley Walker* in 1980) the intensified exploration of the nuclear theme which was to be found, during the eighties, in all of the arts. And in criticism. In 1984 Cornell University hosted a number of scholars at a colloquium whose aim was to examine the role of critical theory in a nuclear age. "Nuclear criticism" was christened and inaugurated in a special issue of *Diacritics* made up of a selection of papers from the colloquium. The work that followed in nuclear criticism is already too variegated, and too extensive, to sum up readily: the *Newsletter* of the International Society for the Study of Nuclear Texts and Contexts has half a hundred listings in every issue. In all of these ways, then, this book is a product of its time.

Of course, that time has changed now, in the early nineties, from what it was in the eighties; and the changes are likely to be retrospective as well, changing the ways that we read the changes we believe ourselves already to have passed through. As I write this, in January of 1991, it is a year since I was told that I was working on a passé problem: the Berlin wall had fallen, and a process of disarmament had been set in motion. Today the expectations of that time seem ironic. Images of war fill the television screens, and the use of nuclear weapons is talked of as an "option." When this book is published, that way of talking will seem either an ominous foreshadowing or a delusory bugbear. And that verdict will change again as these words are read at various points in time. What will not change is the presence of the bomb itself: a new possibility has come into the world, and it will remain a part of our possible selves. To calculate its stock only on the basis of today's news is to practice the thinnest sort of pragmatism.

On the other hand, it is perhaps a natural impulse to interpret the nuclear dilemma on the basis of tonight's television images. Whatever those images may be, they are more comprehensible than those associated with nuclear disaster—images which, at the deepest level, turn upon themselves to question the very notion of imaging itself. The hypothetical space of nuclear disaster cannot be inhabited by the imagination, as Robert Jay Lifton has observed. No more can its hypothetical time: Richard Klein has written a number of provocative essays on the paradoxes of nuclear temporality. For most people the single most disturbing fact about nuclear temporality is the instantaneousness of nuclear annihilation. If, as we are coming to understand, time is running out for the environment, time is at least still running. Nuclear disaster, on the other hand, is capable of occurring at any moment, in a moment, with no time even for an explanation of why there is no time. Believing that this will not happen—as perhaps that which is life affirming in us has to—we are yet affected by the very undecidedness of this outcome, the radical instability that underlies our lives. A hovering anxiety characterizes the nuclear age. When it is diffused by hopeful developments, the diffusion is only, as it has been all along, into more indirect manifestations, a subtle working in our cultural unconscious: I am thinking of the world of Don Delillo's *White Noise*. So the question of nuclear holocaust becomes a question about how our minds work, consciously or unconsciously. And if, as Lacan suggests, the unconscious is structured as a language, it becomes a question about literature, questions literature. Can the unthinkable be written? Or, as some thinkers would have it, can anything *else* ever be written? And will that writing only record the nuclear age, or does it have the capacity to change it? This book about books must ask itself the same sort of question. Sooner or later it will be a historical study. Perhaps it already is. But the questions that were initiated by the birth of the bomb will not leave us: we can't go home again.

However, it may be that a new homeland, as Ernst Bloch would call it, will be attained, and attained with the help of literature. As one of Philip Roth's characters says, "Literature got me into this, and literature is gonna have to get me out" (Roth 1974, 174).

Indeed, literature was complicit in the nuclear age from the start: the nuclear bomb was initiated by, among other things, a novel. H. G. Wells dedicated *The World Set Free,* published in 1913, to Frederick Soddy, a pioneer in the exploration of radioactivity. Using Soddy's research as a base, Wells predicted the advent of artificial radioactivity in 1933, the year in which it actually took place; and he foresaw its use for what he named the "atomic bomb." In Wells's novel these bombs are used in a world war that erupts in midcentury and is so catastrophic that a world government is formed, initiating a new age powered by the peaceful use of the atom. The physicist Leo Szilard, a longtime admirer of Wells, read this novel in 1932, the year before he first intuited the possibility of a nuclear chain reaction. The novel seems to have become part of his own mental chain reaction, one that took place at an almost unconscious level during the spring that Szilard spent at the Strand Palace Hotel in London, by his own admission doing nothing. He would only monopolize the bath from around nine in the morning to noon, since "there is no place as good to think as a bathtub" (Szilard 1978, 19). The theories that resulted from this prolonged immersion were introduced by references to Wells; and Szilard, having realized the atomic bomb, spent the rest of his life trying to realize the world government that, in the Wells novel, was its consequence.

The bomb continues to be *"fabulously textual,* through and through," as Jacques Derrida says in the most influential essay in nuclear criticism, the one that indeed may be said to have initiated nuclear criticism. "No Apocalypse, Not Now" does not deny the reality of the nuclear weapons that are stockpiled everywhere. But it does argue that a nuclear war has not taken place—the bombings of 1945, in Derrida's opinion, ending a "classical" war rather than setting off a nuclear one. And if it has not taken place one can *only* talk or write about it: "the terrifying reality of the nuclear conflict can only be the signified referent, never the real referent (present or past) of a discourse or text" (Derrida 1984, 23).

Yet, lacking one reality—that of total nuclear war—the fabulously textual version of nuclear war is capable of generating another: "'Reality,' let's say the encompassing institution of the nuclear age, is constructed by the fable." That institution is "techno-militaro-politico-diplomatic," but it is even more encompassing than that. For all these competencies have to take into account, as part of their competency, margins of error, of incompetency, of bluff, fiction, fear, panic—every wrinkle of the human psyche. Thus the binary opposition between competency and incompetency begins to blur, as does a more venerable opposition: "one can no longer oppose belief and science, *doxa* and *épistémè*, once one has reached the decisive place of the nuclear age" (Derrida 1984, 24). Nuclear strategy mingles science with beliefs about others' beliefs, and of course about others' science, and one's own, in a proliferating and paradoxical network of speculation which yet constitutes our reality.

If in such ways nuclear war is dominated by textuality, is in a sense created by it, we have an extreme example of the dominance of the signifier over the signified. The title of this book may be read according to this formulation, as if there were an invisible bar between the "Letter" and the "Bomb" that is its ostensible signified. But this bar, far from being a bar to our understanding, can support the claim of possible understanding. The dominance of the signifier means we know who is in charge, or what. The paradoxes of textuality seem safely distant, even familiar: we have an updated version of the pen being mightier than the sword. Crossing the bar would mean admitting that the letter's existence itself is at stake in a far more volatile power dynamic. Derrida admits as much in "No Apocalypse," analyzing literature as an archival institution that, like the nuclear age itself, is fabulously textual, without any referent outside of the words by which it constitutes itself. Consequently, there would be nothing by which it could reconstruct its past if the bomb that is hypothetically constructed in textuality explodes in reality. "The hypothesis of this total destruction watches over deconstruction, it guides its footsteps," asserts Derrida (1984, 27). Here global annihilation acts like a parent (absent father, father of absence?) hovering over an infant criticism as it takes its first faltering steps: bomb over letter, in effect. We might also say that there is a bomb within the letter: words explode. They do this despite themselves, as deconstruction has demonstrated. But texts may also write *towards* explosion. For Kafka, this (and not the archival institution) was the distinguishing mark of literature. Literature is that which creates the question, including in that question literature itself. The same sort of thing can be said of the bomb, of course. The questioning then becomes a reciprocal one.

This book attempts, if not to fix the role of literature in such a dynamic, at least to indicate that it *has* a role. Derrida describes the nuclear situation as a "limit case in which the limit itself is suspended, in which therefore the *krinein,* crisis, decision itself, and choice are being subtracted from us, are abandoning us like the remainder of that subtraction" (Derrida 1984, 22–23). The bar between "Letter" and "Bomb" would thus become a minus sign. What is left of literature in the nuclear age? Is the "remainder"— that which for Derrida is uncountable, unaccountable in the text—destined to abandon us along with the remnants of our choice? Or does the word, even as it explodes, open new energies in us? There is no simple answer to these questions. Even to hear their reverberation requires the full process of a text, in all its intricate fissions and fusions.

Of course, in phrasing the matter like this I have tilted it toward another reading of the title. *Letter Bomb* is a package that is meant to explode. There are many tensions between the thinkers I deal with here, primarily Derrida, Jacques Lacan, René Girard, Maurice Blanchot, Ernst Bloch. And it is less my purpose to reconcile those tensions than to exacerbate them. Not only are these thinkers played against each other, but against works of literature (occasionally film or music) explicitly dealing with the nuclear theme: works by Russell Hoban, Thomas Pynchon, Bernard Malamud, Denis Johnson, Tim O'Brien, and others. These become the nuclear testing ground of theory. As the book progresses, it also regresses: doubling back upon itself, repeating with variations, coming at the same point from another angle, reinterpreting recurrent images. In these ways the book accumulates a charge that may take it beyond the position I myself have taken, or the points I have made.

In diagrams of nuclear warheads a tiny speck is labeled "initiator." If we seek its analogue in the letter we may ask either what initiated the letter, the literary work; or we can ask what is initiated by it. In the first case we have an endless recession, or a past origin initiated retrospectively by the present. In the second case we have something more useful; for although we may maintain that there are no beginnings, we cannot deny that there are changes, differences; and some differences are more critical than others, setting off further changes. Derrida's influential essay is structured as a series of "seven missiles, seven missives," with "no apocalypse," in the sense of ultimate revelation, at the destination of either letter or bomb. Perhaps so. But in "the nuclear age" (a process, not a static entity) we may find motion more useful than revelation. The real race is not between superpowers but between proliferation of a mechanistic, supremely paradoxical system of armament and the consciousness of its creators, of what Derrida says "is still, now and then, called human." Literature has its part to play here, as does criticism. This essay in nuclear criticism is the product of a chain reaction between many books. Its aim is to initiate more books, at a time in which both letter and bomb continue their tendencies to critical mass.

1 DECONSTRUCTION AND DETOUR

Post Nuclear Post Card

"What is closest *must* be avoided, by virtue of its very proximity," Derrida has said in *The Post Card*. "It must be kept at a distance, it must be warned" (1987, 263). The aphoristic ring of this invites applications beyond those of its context (Freud's debt to Nietzsche, psychology's debt to philosophy). What is closest to us, then, may be precisely that which we do not think about, that which we call the unthinkable. The suspended and continually postponed moment of nuclear annihilation affects all the moments of our lives in ways we are not fully aware of and cannot be, never having known any other mode of existence. Like nuclear testing itself, its psychological effects have gone underground. We may detect its traces, however, in the most apparently remote areas—such as literary theory, and specifically Derrida's *Post Card*. Derrida's text reveals a nuclear element beneath its leading metaphors and preoccupations; in so doing it raises the larger issue of the relationship of literary theory, and of literature, to the nuclear moment. If nuclear holocaust is that which must be "kept at a distance" and "warned" (*averti*), in what sense are we to take these words? Is it that literature holds our own horror at a safe distance from us, domesticating the Beast by penning it into narrative structures? Or does literature, theoretically at least, help to keep the forces of nuclearism itself at a distance by warning us of its nature and our own? And how is that warning to be accomplished if not by closing the distance through some form of words? It is not a matter of simply choosing an answer, though choice is at the root of the nuclear situation. Answers and questions interpenetrate here, quite as much as texts do.

The problematic nature of Derrida's *Post Card,* like that of any text, exists in conjunction with other texts, which may also be described as post cards. "A post card," Derrida explains, "is never but a piece of a letter, a letter that puts itself, at the very second of the pickup, *into pieces*" (1987, 67). The letter that deconstructs itself is *littera,* the literary, literature itself. So if we are to pick up on the questions that have just been asked about a certain "literature," it is fitting that we do so through its pieces. We may begin by shuffling the cards, adding to Derrida's *Post Card* two other texts with postal preoccupations: David Brin's novel of postnuclear life, *The Postman,* and Peter Townsend's nonfiction account of *The Postman of Nagasaki.*

1

Derrida's book was galvanized by a chance encounter with a post card on sale at the Bodleian Library. The card reproduces a thirteenth-century picture of Plato and Socrates in which, much to Derrida's delight, Plato stands behind the seated Socrates, apparently dictating what he shall write (fig. 1). This image illustrates Derrida's notion that knowledge constantly creates its own presumed origins. The image, like the idea, reverses the usual concepts of transmission—concepts that are an aspect of the post card itself, quite apart from its particular image. For any post card is part of a system of relays for carrying and delivering meaning. Addressed and signed, it assumes an identity at either end of the communication process: a "sender" and an "addressee." Derrida would question the stability and coherence of both of these; he would question the truth that is presumably communicated, as well as the nature of that communication. In this view the post card and the postal system emblematize the very idea of logocentrism, of a stable meaning that inhabits the letter.

Yet in another view the post card is opposed to the letter, is the very emblem of that which challenges logocentrism. Raising the problem of the relation between image and text, it vividly reminds us of its two-sidedness. "Wish you were here" is the classic message of the post card, referring to an image on its back (or is it front?). That message can be read metaphysically, in terms of desire and presence. Where is the "here"? On the other side of the text, or situated within it, by it? Does the represented scene generate the wish, or does the wish generate its necessary referent in the scene? What is the relation of that scene to the scene of writing? All of these problems are opened up by the post card, and are presented openly—exposed to anyone's gaze—in contrast to the closed letter. More fragmentary than letters, or than literature, post cards vividly remind us of that which is between them. They are multiplied—same image, different texts—and disseminated. For if the postal system is logocentric, it is also disseminatory; that letters or cards will go astray is always possible, and therefore for Derrida necessary. This is logically implicit in the nature of a postal relay itself. If the letter were absolutely stable, indivisible, its destination and its origin would be one and the same. But with division in time and space comes the necessary possibility that a letter will not reach its destination. In that case it can become a "dead letter" or, more fruitfully, may be stamped "Return to Sender." What is initiated in the latter case is a "return inquiry" reversing the sequence of transmission or tradition, as it is reversed in the picture of Socrates and Plato.

Such a return inquiry is a prominent feature of most nuclear novels. Typically, these are set in a time after a nuclear war has taken place; it is through deciphering its traces that we learn about the nature of that war and of our own situation before its outbreak. So it is in Brin's *Postman,* which is constructed on many of the same preoccupations as those of Derrida. From the

1 The Post Card. MS Ashmole 304, Fol. 31v (detail). Plato and Socrates, the frontispiece of *Prognostica Socratis basilei,* an English fortune-telling book of the thirteenth century by Matthew Paris. Illustration courtesy of the Bodleian Library, University of Oxford.

first page these are literary preoccupations. Gordon Krantz, a survivor in postnuclear North America, is dragging himself through the underbrush when he has a peculiar backflash: *words on a page.* The strangeness of this perception to a man who has spent "half a lifetime in the wilderness, most of it struggling to survive," is itself strange to a reader who is at that moment staring at words on a page—words that transmit a future flashing back to a past that is our present. Transmission, in many senses, is problematized from the start. During his travels Krantz comes across a dead mailman and a bag of dead letters.

For his own purposes he takes the uniform and the bag, with unexpected consequences: he finds himself hailed by the isolated communities he visits as the first sign of a restored social order. Some of the letters in the bag prove deliverable; new letters are given to him. Assenting to this fiction, Krantz finds it beginning to turn into a fact. Other mail carriers join him, creating a network between the semifeudal villages of postnuclear Oregon. And Krantz finds himself leading the resistance to marauding survivalists, taking over from an effete culture powerless to defend itself owing to its trust in a very different sort of system. In effect, the authority of the postal system is pitted against another authority, that of a gigantic supercomputer maintained by a kind of priesthood. Rather as in *The Wizard of Oz,* this turns out to be a sham, a sterile fiction whose centralizing nature lacks the vitality of the proliferating system of postal relays.

Brin's novel, like Derrida's theory, thus underscores the importance of the postal principle. Moreover, as a fiction about the postnuclear world, it enacts the same reverse transmission as that depicted on the Bodleian post card: grandsons dictate to grandfathers what they will have said. A post–nuclear war narrative is addressed to, posted to, those who live in a prewar condition. To the degree that this is a didactic fiction, its aim is to initiate a "return inquiry" into the origins of that postnuclear world in the world we are inhabiting now.

The fact that all this takes place through a work of literature is problematic from Derrida's point of view. "Literature has always appeared unacceptable to me," he says, "a scandal, the moral fault *par excellence,* and like a post card seeking to pass itself off as something else, as a true letter" (1987, 38). Like a post card, literature, the supposedly true letter, is two-sided. Looking at it one way, it is constructed on the postal principle, to such a degree that Derrida can claim that "the end of a postal epoch is doubtless also the end of literature" (1987, 104). Yet literature has a reverse side by which all its patterns of transmission are exploded: Blanchot would call this aspect of literature "the disaster." Accepting this word, indeed reveling in it (1987, 108), Derrida has elsewhere specified a nuclear disaster, asserting that "literature belongs to this nuclear epoch," and indeed that "literature has always belonged to the nuclear epoch" (1984, 27). This is so to the degree that literature and nuclear holocaust share "the historical and ahistorical horizon of an absolute self-destructibility without apocalypse, without revelation of its own truth, without absolute knowledge" (1984, 27). The nuclear component of literature is a figure of speech, of course, but no more innocent than any such figure—as is demonstrated by a passage in *The Post Card,* a passage from a letter, in which the figure becomes disturbingly literal. Derrida, or his persona, is taking issue with his lover's expressed intention to arrive at a "determination":

> The only possible "determination" for me—and moreover I obey it every moment without seeming to: burn everything, forget everything, in order to see if the force of starting again without a trace, without an opened path
> [Here a blank, a portion destroyed by censorship or by fire.
> He resumes:]
> The symbol? A great holocaustic fire, a burn-everything into which we would throw finally, along with our entire memory, our names, the letters, photos, small objects, keys, fetishes, etc. And if nothing remains
> [Another blank; and then]
> What do you think? I await your response. (1987, 40)

This is what Barbara Freeman has called nuclear desire: not only the secret wish for nuclear holocaust but the fusion of that wish with erotic desire. Both forms of burning underlie the long first part of *The Post Card,* the "Envois." These are a series of letters, or post cards, addressed to a lover. "You might consider them," Derrida suggests, "as the remainders of a recently destroyed correspondence. Destroyed by fire or by that which figuratively takes its place" (1987, 3). The fire is indeed figurative, in a number of ways; but it is not more figurative than the correspondence itself, generated by Derrida to make a point, or rather a whole series of points. If figurative, the "Envois" are as much a product of literature as that mailbag found in a nuclear aftermath in David Brin's novel.

To these two collections of singed letters we may add a third and real one. Fifteen-year-old Sumiteru, the so-called *Postman of Nagasaki,* was on his morning rounds when the bomb hit. Struggling to his feet with the skin of his back hanging in sheets from his waist, his first thought was for his letters. During two days of agony he refused to be parted from his postbag and finally handed in his letters to the post office. Sumiteru, so faithful to the postal principle, became its incarnation. His back, healed but bearing hideous scars, became a more significant message than any of his letters. As if he were a human post card, the bomb had written on his back. This image fuses with a number of Derrida's preoccupations in *The Post Card:* with scars (1987, 40, 48) and above all with the back, with knowledge obtained from the back. Epistemologically, Derrida claims, "there is only the *back,* seen from the back, in what is written, such is the final word" (1987, 48). If it is the final word, it is also perhaps the word that was in the beginning according to St. John, the Word that is God, the same God who refused to show his face to Moses, saying only "you shall see my back parts." This is the retroactive nature of our knowledge, and this is how we come to know. Sumiteru, a simple man, comes to know this as well as anybody. At first attempting to move into the future by putting the horrors of the bomb behind him, he learns paradoxically to face his own back. He learns that not only his future but that of the world depends on how it reads its past, what it chooses to have originated in that blinding moment at Nagasaki. One day, then, he deliberately takes off his shirt at a crowded public beach, thus admitting that his body itself is a message whose meaning has yet to be made, initiating a perpetual return inquiry.

We have three versions of the post card in the bag so far:

philosophical, literary, somatic. To these we may add a fourth: the nuclear missile itself, which is obviously used as a counter for communications in nuclear diplomacy. Arms talk. As Derrida has depicted it in "No Apocalypse, Not Now," a missile is a missive. Two-sided as any post card, its nature is paradoxical—like Derrida's convoluted philosophy, or Brin's predictive fiction, or Sumiteru's psychology. In deterrence diplomacy, the missile is aimed, but its real aim is precisely not to attain that toward which it is aimed. The more believable it is that the missile will reach its target the less likely it becomes that it will do so; its aim becomes false the more it rings true. Paradoxical as this seems, it is not so different from the cautionary future of Brin's novel, also a form of deterrence strategy. Activated, the missile becomes even more paradoxical. If a missive, it bears a message that, upon reaching its destination, annihilates it; in a sense, then, it can never reach that destination. It can never deliver a message that is annihilated along with the addressee and, quite likely, the sender. Thus the tenets of deconstruction are validated: a literal and all-encompassing disaster enacts the "disaster" that is a figurative way of speaking about the annihilation coeval with every act of creation. But awareness of that theoretical "disaster" is different from the nuclear disaster that will put an end to all awareness, that will close down all the deconstructive processes that endlessly postpone closure. There may not even be time to say "I told you so."

This, if it could be spoken, would be the classic final word—but, significantly, it reverses itself, turns back. Predicting a future, we thus find ourselves turned back to the past, which is our present, and our present task to interpret. This is a pattern repeated in Sumiteru's life, in Brin's science fiction, and in Derrida's original post card, which incidentally is the frontispiece of a fortune-telling book. We can tell our nuclear fortune, the fate of the earth, only through a return inquiry. And this concept of the return inquiry is the most valuable part of Derrida's thinking in this area. All nuclear missiles (missives) are stamped "Return to

Sender," but we may interpret that in more than one way. On the one hand, the missiles may engage in what the Pentagon graciously calls a "reciprocal exchange." On the other hand, the missiles may be returned to their origins in the senders, that is, in us. There, if our minds can find ways to free ourselves from bonds, or binds, that we ourselves have created, the dismantling of the machines follows as a matter of course.

Used in this way, deconstruction opposes destruction and opposes its own tendency to nuclear desire. The return inquiry, however, is not a straightforward route, or a simple one, or even one that needs to reach its (reverse) destination. We are dealing with many post cards here. Each of these interacts with the others within the postal network; each, to the degree that it approaches its destination, will cause the others to go astray. If David Brin manages to get his message across, the nuclear missile will never be sent; if Derrida convinces us, we will distrust our reading of Brin, or we will simply distrust reading; if Sumiteru uncovers his back at a crowded beach, he is showing the onlookers that nuclear war is not just, as Derrida claims, "fabulously textual"; if the missile delivers, all messages go astray forever, never to reach their destinations. Of course, missiles too may go astray: "an absolute missile does not abolish chance," Derrida reminds us in "No Apocalypse" (1984, 29); its launching may itself be due to a stray chance. But in the view I am proposing, "going astray" is not just a matter of chance, a kind of willful jog in the system like that in the Lucretian universe. Quite as much as from some flaw in the message itself, or in the postal system, a message is deflected by other messages. What is stamped upon time, Derrida says at one point, "composes itself with billions of other obliterating positions, impositions, or superimpositions" (1987, 101).

2

Within this complex postal system, what role can be played by literature, that post card that claims the completeness of the letter? Does literature have the capacity to leave its stamp upon time, or to ensure the continuance even of the concept of time, beyond the nuclear age? The question is similar to that posed by the second part of *The Post Card,* entitled "To Speculate—on 'Freud.'" In the "Envois," Derrida had stated that "the post is always *en reste,* and always *restante*" (1987, 191). The postal term, with its connotations of inconclusiveness, of waiting, is linked to Derrida's notion of *restance,* that which remains unaccounted for in any text. Now he states, "I would like to pursue the analysis of *restance* in order to attempt to recognize, using this example, the conditions for the fictional, and for that type of fiction called, confusedly sometimes, literature" (1987, 262). Faulted by ambiguity, the sentence splits along that fault line. To speak of "the conditions for the fictional" promises, perhaps, an analysis of those aspects of fiction, such as *restance,* which are excluded by and underlie its specious existence. Or it promises an investigation of the conditions that would have to be met if literature—"inadmissible literature" he calls it at one point—were to become, conditionally, admissible. Or it goes beyond this either/or.

The second part of *The Post Card* is a reading of Freud's *Beyond the Pleasure Principle* in terms of Derrida's postal principle. It emphasizes particularly the *fort:da* scene, in which Freud's grandson Ernst throws a bobbin on a string away (*fort!*) from him and then draws it back until it reappears (*da!*). This scene may be thought of as the text's "icon," in Derrida's own terms. "Everything I write is legendary, a more or less elliptical, redundant, or untranslatable legend, caption, *of the picture.* Of the icon which is found on the back of the text and watches over it" (1987, 122). The terms are, of course, those of the post card; and the *fort:da* scene itself, in Derrida's reading, has postal implications. In its original context, the scene is notoriously problematic: it is, for instance, simultaneously an example of the repetition compulsion that appears to challenge the supremacy of the pleasure principle, and an example of the mastery of painful events (in this case disappearance, absence of the mother) through an artifice that subsumes them *under* the pleasure principle. As Derrida reads it, the scene's implications exfoliate even more. The movement of the *fort:da* is also that of Freud—or rather of "Freud," the man who has become an idea, the idea of the psychoanalytic movement itself. That movement is relinquished by Freud to his intellectual grandsons, only to be pulled back by the master, by the very idea of mastery. And his speculative writing—writing without a thesis or with "athesis"—constantly undoes itself and constantly finds itself again. The *fort:da* has to do with the "posting" of an intellectual tradition, then, and reminds us how far from straightforward that delivery is. But what will concern us most here is the simple statement that "the *fort:da* is a narrative" (1987, 370).

By this, what is being said about narrative? The scene, according to Derrida, is "concerned with the theme of repetition, of relation, of the narrative as a return to a previous state" (1987, 370). "Relation" punningly reminds us of the network of connections assumed in the telling of any tale. "Repetition" in this context has been explicated most clearly by Peter Brooks in his reading of "Freud's Masterplot," as he calls *Beyond the Pleasure Principle:*

> Repetition in all its literary manifestations may in fact work as a "binding," a binding of textual energies that allows them to be mastered by putting them into serviceable form within the energetic economy of the narrative. Serviceable form must in this case mean perceptible form: repetition, repeat, recall, symmetry, all these journeys back in the text, returns to and returns of, that allow us to bind one textual moment to another in terms of similarity and substitution rather than mere contiguity. (1977, 289–90)

Binding allows plot to emerge out of "mere contiguity." In this sense "repetition is mastery" (Brooks 1977, 286), and it may be linked to Freud's preliminary hypothesis that the *fort:da* is an attempt to master, by replaying it, the mother's absence. In another sense, Derrida's sense in "Ellipsis," "pure repetition, were it to change neither thing nor sign, carries with it an unlimited power of perversion and subversion" (1978a, 296). Derrida thus moves away from "the classical distinction, within repetition, of the repeated and the repeating" which assumes that "a narrative relates something that would be previous and foreign to itself"—something that, by that relation, is mastered. Instead he reminds us that there are cases when, "according to a logic that is other, and non-classical, repetition is 'original', and induces, through an unlimited propagation of itself, a general deconstruction" (1987, 351–52). Repetition, then, and relation; and finally, there is the notion of the narrative as a "return to a previous state." This identifies the course of the narrative with Freud's *Umweg*.

The *Umweg* is the detour that, Freud speculates, the organism takes in order to arrive at its own "proper" death: the death that is immanent in the byways of its life; the death that is the state previous to its existence. It must draw back that state to itself, rather as Ernst draws in his wooden bobbin. Only now it is absence itself (*fort*) that is brought home (*da*) by the so-called death instinct. For Derrida, Freud's notions of *Umweg* in *Beyond the Pleasure Principle* can be extrapolated into a deconstructionist version of the idea.

> The *Umweg* of the first chapter would constitute only an internal, secondary, and conditional modification of the absolute and unconditional *Umweg*. It would be in the service of the general *Umweg*, of the (no) step of the detour [*pas de détour*] which always leads back to death. *Leads back*—here again it is not a question of going, but of coming back [*revenir*]. It is this double determination that I had assigned to the "word" *différance* with an *a*. (1987, 354)

All these comings and goings, and the questionings thereof, relate the *Umweg* to the *fort:da* scene. As for the relation to narrative, that has as much to do with narrative's construction as with its deconstruction: the two are part of the same process. For Brooks and others, plot begins with a stimulation from quiescence into desire; moves through the middle's vacillating space of postponement; and finds its closure once again in quiescence. But that quiescence, the narrative's death, must be of a kind that is proper to it, must not be foreclosed. As with *Umweg,* the aim has been to achieve the organism's proper death. The postponement, whether conceived as spatial or temporal, allows the "proper" to precipitate out of its vacillations. It gives the necessary time for the death instinct to find the form that is proper to the organism, to the narrative conceived of as organism.

The statement just made raises, of course, a number of theoretical questions: the nature of the "proper," for instance, linked with problems of identity and destination; or whether "the" narrative exists as such, when it may compose itself out of a polyphony of narrative voices. Without resolving these questions theoretically, Maggie Gee has exploited them artistically in her nuclear novel, *The Burning Book.* The novel is a family chronicle spanning three generations which is abruptly terminated by nuclear holocaust. It makes the point, made by Robert Jay Lifton among others, that nuclear death is not merely the untold multiplication of human death but is a change in its nature: it bereaves the dying of their proper deaths, of death given meaning in the context of time, of narrative time, of chronicle. "We live our lives as a tale that is told," says the psalmist—but in the bomb's story beginning and end collapse into one blank quiescence.

In the telling of her tale Gee lets other tales intrude, other voices be heard: "I'm trying to tell a straight story, just like everyone else. But voices keep interrupting. Cries thrown back from the future" (1983, 113). These interruptions are not so much foreshadowings as postshadowings. Nuclear events cast their shadows backward; the usual patterns of transmission are thrown into question, including above all narrative transmission. Gee's book is postal, then, in the sense that it deals with its own posting in a network of messages which includes nuclear

missiles. Rather like Derrida's "Envois," it exhibits the fissures in
its text:

> *with such a hubbub outside, great cracks appear in my novel*
> other novels do better, build us a paper home
> but *Japanese walls like pages*   (1983, 52)

In both cases, the gaps in the text imply an ultimate burning. In
Derrida's case, the destruction is selective: the author decides
what shall be retained, what shall be obliterated. Moreover, "Envois" pertains to a *book:* it serves as a preface to the already
determined reading of Freud which follows. Print on a page—the
sign of the prenuclear world—remains, *restante.* In Gee's case,
we are invited to become aware of the book not just as symbolic
of the archival idea but as physical object. We are invited not just
to read about nuclear fire in its pages but to see those pages burn;
the last few pages are literally blackened. A point is being made:
the effect of nuclear holocaust is as unthinkable as the coming of
real fire to the fictive world that is consumed by it. Gee's larger
theme, however, is the relation between the fire and the fiction,
nuclearism and narrative. That relation is not over when the
book, and its world, are over. In an envoi "Against Ending" words
disseminate on the page and take the increasingly clear shape of
birds (doves of peace? postal pigeons?): "words beat on against
death." In this resistance Gee is in accord with a comment by
Derrida to the effect that the social function of literature and
criticism is, Scheherazade-like, to keep us talking in order to
defer the apocalypse (Salusinszky 1987, 21–22).

Yet a certain *kind* of "talking" (here read "writing") is needed
if literature is to be admissible. While Gee burns the physical
book, Derrida's ideal, or that of his narrator, is a language that
burns:

> I would like to write you so simply, so simply, so simply. With-
> out having anything ever catch the eye, excepting yours alone,
> and what is more while erasing all the traits, even the most in-
> apparent ones, the ones that mark the tone, or the belonging to

a genre (the letter for example, or the post card), so that above
all the language remains self-evidently secret, as if it were being invented at every step, and as if it were burning immediately, as soon as any third party would set eyes on it. (1987, 11)

Of course "Envois" itself exemplifies such a writing. It can be
read as an epistolary novel, a novel both of and about letters. And
the way that it is written is the most important thing about it:
"you know that I never write *on* anything, not even on the post
card or on telethisthat. Even if I feign writing about it, and no
matter what I say, before all else I am seeking to produce effects"
(1987, 113). This statement may be compared with the judgment
pronounced by the same voice later: "Until the end of time, the
ignoble descendance will know how to get effects from everything while washing their hands of it. To know how still *to get
an effect* from suffering or from love is the very essence of the
ignoble: not to know how to burn [A gap follows in the text.]"
(1987, 236).

The text is "burned" here—but without success. The "third
party," working in a void, goes on to read it; for the void is far
from empty. The reader irresistibly constructs a completion, or
several alternate completions. Is the burning here a commonplace one, that of love or suffering or the two combined? And are
we merely being told to "suffer in silence," avoiding postures of
self-pity and/or noble endurance? Or is the burning that which
destroyed the correspondence of which this letter is a remainder—thus, an actual fire "or that which figuratively takes its
place" (1987, 3)? What takes its place? Something akin to Blanchot's "disaster"? Yet that disaster befalls all notions of the subject, and the grammatical structure here ("to know how to burn")
empowers the (noble) subject. Unless the burning is passive, an
acquiescence—which is disturbingly close to the action, or non-
action, of "washing their hands of it." Finally, the nuclear element hangs suspended here, among other possibilities. And in
retrospect the opening of this passage ("until the end of time")

becomes more than a standard rhetorical flourish. The passage passes through "ignoble descendance," which is a condition in time, the condition of being in a time that is postoriginal, to an ability "to know how to burn," which will take place precisely at the end of time, in real fire.

These are all speculations; they do not come to a point of decision. But the point here is undecidability itself, a "burning" of logocentrism which is, nevertheless, an *effect*. In effect, we have read the unreadable, though to be sure in an unfamiliar mode of reading, produced by an unfamiliar mode of writing. Ignoble or not, it is inevitable to produce effects of one kind or another; and this kind of language, in the very act of disclaiming, produces its effects: the effect of *différance,* it may be; the effect of postal dissemination; the literary effect of that which opposes the letter, opposes literature.

Through the practice of his essay, Derrida seems to be suggesting a literature to oppose and replace an "inadmissible" classical one—a literature that in the terms of his essay may be called "speculative." This term is capable of a panoply of readings, and that is one of the essay's points. On the one hand, speculation is economic, capitalistic: it can be applied to a sort of trading in ideas (or in names such as "Freud") which seeks the ultimate control that is the aim of metaphysical speculation; and (to bring in further associations) it valorizes the gaze of an all-seeing subject who sees, as with Hegel, in all things the mirror of himself. On the other hand, speculation is gambling, risk taking; if a monetary metaphor must be applied, let it be, as Brian Rotman has suggested, that of futures trading, in which shares are sold at their hypothetical future value (in contrast to paper money, which points backwards to material guarantees of its value deposited in a vault). The postmodern text, says Rotman, is "forced as a sign to engage in the creation of its own signified—one written in the only terms available to it, that is, future states of itself" (1987, 101). The comparison restores to speculation its hypothetical quality.

If a speculative literature is what Derrida is calling for, the model for it is both Freud's way of writing *Beyond the Pleasure Principle* and Derrida's way of reading it. Both writers inhabit the following passage from "Envois":

> The master-thinkers are also masters of the post. Knowing well how to play with the *poste restante.* Knowing how not to be there and how to be strong for not being there right away. Knowing how not to deliver on command, how to wait and to make wait, for as long as what there is that is strongest within one demands—and to the point of dying without mastering anything of the final destination. (1987, 191)

Without seeking for a "final destination," we should note the terms in which Derrida, at the end of *To Speculate—on "Freud,"* sums up the experience of Freud's book; they are among other things the terms of the repetitive *fort:da:*

> Is what we have retained from *Beyond* . . . anything other than a rhythm, the rhythm of a step which always *comes back* [*revient*], which again has just left? Which has always just left again? And if there is a theme, in the interpretation of this piece, a theme rather than a thesis, it is perhaps *rhythmos,* and the rhythm of the theme no less than the theme of a rhythm. (1987, 405–6)

Juxtaposing this passage to an earlier one, we can see the significance of this theme to Derrida's work through his analysis of its significance to Freud's:

> Freud is preparing a map of routes and a record of *différances* of rhythm. A differantial, and not an "alternating" rhythm, as the French translation gives "Zauderrhythmus" ["vacillating"]. *Zaudern* is to hesitate, certainly, but it is above all to *temporize,* to defer, to delay. One group of drives rushes forward in order to reach the final aim of life as quickly as possible. But, division of labor, another group comes back [*revient*] to the start of the same path (*dieses Weges zurück*) in order to go over the route and "so prolong the journey." (1987, 361–62)

All this relates, of course, to Derrida's comment on the social function of literature and criticism—but not unproblematically. The problems are reflected in the very terminology of the passages cited. To "prolong the journey" by resisting the death instinct, the lure of nuclear desire, is no doubt noble. But in Derrida's version it may rapidly become indistinguishable from temporizing, delaying, vacillating—"to the point of dying." For launched missiles will not wait for us to finish our sentences, sentencing ourselves to death. Rather the missiles must be returned to their senders even before they are posted, and something in the *timbre* of the sender's mind must make it impossible for them ever to be posted. Quite simply, we must change. Einstein's well-known words return to us like a phase of the *fort:da* itself: "The unleashed power of the atom has changed everything save our modes of thinking, and we thus drift toward unparalleled catastrophes" (1975, 376).

To break the vacillating drift that is one form of deconstructive reading it is advisable to quarrel with its metaphors—the icons that back the text—or at least to indicate that these may be read in alternative ways. This is, after all, exactly what Derrida has done with little Ernst's bobbin. Why not resist, then, the seductive vacillation of the following passage by expropriating its icon?

> We will say that the irresolution of the scene of writing that we
> are reading [Freud's] is that of a *Bindung* which tends,
> stretches itself and ceaselessly posts (sends, detaches, displaces,
> replaces) to the extreme, without conclusion, without solution,
> without acting, and without a final orgasm (rather a series of
> orgasmic tremors, of enjoyments deferred as soon as obtained,
> posted in their very instance). (1987, 397)

Derrida seizes upon Freud's word *Bindung,* referring to the binding of psychic energy, and connects it to the French *bander,* to get an erection. The sex here is far from apocalyptic and might be diagnosed as a stubborn desire for phallic mastery, if willed—

or, if not, as a clinical problem. Certainly other forms of sexuality are possible. And because the sexuality here is a metaphor for writing, for reading, for knowing, we are reminded that all these may exist in alternative modes—alternatives that are often expressed in sexual terms, and usually, as here, in male sexual terms.

Beginning with a critique of Peter Brooks's sexual metaphors in "Freud's Masterplot," Susan Winnett has invited us to consider what the shape of narrative would be if it were governed by female sexual models—as indeed it sometimes has been (Mary Shelley and George Eliot are her examples). And even within the male tradition of such narrative-sexual metaphors one may find versions that challenge Derrida's. Take, for instance, this quotation from the foreword to *Women in Love,* a thoroughly "speculative" novel: "Every natural crisis in emotion or understanding comes from this pulsing, frictional to-and-fro which works up to culmination" (Lawrence 1968, 276). The *fort:da* here is not an interminable hesitation, but a rhythm that allows something to happen. It allows one to inhabit the scene of writing long enough for it to take effect. That effect is an explosion that is not mastery of the final destination, but a kind of dying into awareness— an *un*binding of energy rather than a tense and interminable *Bindung.* The metaphor of the explosion is not only sexual but nuclear: the unbinding of energy in the act of reading a text is the result of a disseminatory process in the psyche which is the counterpart of nuclear processes and is capable of countering them.

Another icon of the text occurs immediately after Derrida's discussion of rhythm; it is the image of a person taking a step:

> The most normal step has to bear disequilibrium, within itself, in order to carry itself forward, in order to have itself followed by another one, the same again, that is a step, and so that the other comes back, amounts to [*revienne*] the same, but as other. Before all else limping has to be the very rhythm of the march. (1987, 406)

This description of the speculative step is yet another version of *fort:da*. The fundamental ambivalence of that description is summed up in a punning reference, earlier in the text, to the *pas d'écriture*. From one perspective, this is writing as negation, the absence of the book, endless deferral and disequilibrium, unavoidable disaster. But from another perspective, a step is taken in the very act of falling, and then another, and these steps make up a march that is not exactly the march of progress, riddled as it is with repeated absences, but that somehow works: *ça marche*. The metaphor of motion here may recall Zeno's paradoxes. Our epistemology is baffled; yet something moves, something changes, change is possible. Texts are posted into a network of relays which may well be too intricate to trace, but which nevertheless leaves its traces. In "Envois" we find a quotation from the *Theatetus:* "States of inactivity rot things and destroy them, whereas states of activity preserve them" (1987, 253). In the midst of "Paralysis" (the title of one of Derrida's chapters) there may be motion, a detour around the death instinct. The postal principle, which is a principle of motion, thus becomes also a principle of preservation.

This essay, of course, has been a misreading of its text. And this has been according to the postal principle itself, whereby no letter reaches its final "destination." Rather it relays itself in new forms, in a process akin to that of metaphoric transference: "Each one makes himself into the *facteur,* the postman, of a narrative that he transmits by maintaining what is 'essential' in it: underlined, cut out, translated, commented, edited, taught, reset in a chosen perspective" (1987, 373). This is what Derrida has done with Freud, and what I have done with Derrida. I have asserted that on the other side of *The Post Card* is the icon of a mushroom cloud. If this is not an accurate transmission of Derrida's purposes and ideas, it is for that very reason all the more a transmission. For motion to take place, there must be change. And I have argued the reverse: for change to take place, there must be motion. I have offered neither origin nor ultimate answer. Only a hoary old plea: Keep those cards and letters coming. The postal network can offer a relay to match that of fission and fusion in its intricacy, its energy, its power of slow explosion. This chapter's final word, if there is such a thing, will be Derrida's: "What cannot be said," he says, "above all must not be silenced, but written" (1987, 194).

Circling Ground Zero

Those who watched the first atomic test saw it literally through a glass darkly, holding pieces of smoked glass before their eyes. What they saw then was filtered in other ways too, as they groped for metaphors that would convey it to others, and to themselves. That which had never been seen before had to be translated into a familiar form. In his *Nuclear Fear: A History of Images* (1988) Spencer Weart cites descriptions of the atomic cloud as a geyser, a cauliflower, a raspberry, a convoluting brain; he then examines the mythical associations that caused the term *mushroom cloud* to prevail over these. Similarly, he links the second most common image, the purely conceptual one of the ringed atom, to the iconic force of the mandala. This circular form reappears in cross sections of the bomb (fig. 2) and in diagrams of the blast (fig. 3), where rings of destruction unfold from ground zero. It is from the image of nuclear aftermath that this chapter unfolds in its turn, for the mapping of ground zero incorporates many of the paradoxes of nuclear representation. Whether the attempt to render the unthinkable is visual, philosophical, or narrative, the same icon governs the complexities involved: a circle around a point designated zero.

In the attempt to diagram the effect of a blast, both circumference and center pose problems. Dantean rings, clearly demarcated, mask the fact that destruction is a continuum. Moreover, though diminishing, the continuum extends beyond any presumed containment or closure. The problem of the center is even more complex, as the citizens of Hiroshima discovered when they were discussing plans for a memorial at the site of ground zero. One survivor suggested leaving a large open space where the bomb exploded, an attempt to represent nothingness—because, as he said, "that was what there was" (Lifton and Falk 1982, 108). Whether nothingness "was," whether absence was present in that moment at Hiroshima, and whether it can be re-presented in any form: these are some of the questions circling this point.

Ground zero is itself a somewhat oxymoronic term. Ground melts away at the point of a nuclear explosion, and the figurative ground of our conceptual systems disappears as well, swallowed by the yawning zero. It is that zero, more than anything else, which serves as sign for what is, or is not, at the blast's center. Zero was a locus of paradox and even terror long before it was applied to the center of the nuclear circle. Arithmeticians split over whether zero was a number among other numbers or whether it was somehow outside of the number system. Those who said that zero was outside saw it as the origin of the number system—though the puzzle of how numbers, conceived of as present, could arise out of an absence engendered paradoxes of infinite regression that had as much to do with Zeno as with zero. The enigma of this sign is implied even in its name: ultimately derived from the Hindu *sunya* "void," *zero* evolves by way of the Arabic *cifer* "cypher." And a cypher, while it is a number, can also be a riddle. In a provocative study of zero, Brian Rotman sums up the concept as follows:

> It is this double aspect of zero, as a sign inside the number system and as a meta-sign, a sign-about-signs outside it, that has allowed zero to serve as the site of an ambiguity between an empty character (whose covert mysterious quality survives in the connection between "cyphers" and secret codes), and a character for emptiness, a symbol that signifies nothing. (1987, 13)

The visual form of that symbol is significant, for it is of course a circle around an emptiness. Ground zero, then, the center of the nuclear circle, recapitulates in its sign the problem of the whole—whether the nuclear blast can be said to have a center, if by center we mean a point at which its presence originated. Ground zero reiterates the arithmetic concept of zero as origin, but with a perverse twist: what originates is an expanding and fading absence. In any variation or version, the center point of a circle, even while posing a problem in representation, may represent another problem, that of the origin.

1

It is this problem that Derrida confronts in his pivotal essay "Structure, Sign and Play in the Discourse of the Human Sciences." Early in the essay he discusses the relation between a structure and its origin, using terms in which we can detect the image we have been examining:

> Structure—or rather the structurality of structure—although it has always been at work, has always been neutralized or reduced, and this by a process of giving it a center or of referring it to a point of presence, a fixed origin. The function of this center was not only to orient, balance, and organize the structure—one cannot in fact conceive of an unorganized structure—but above all to make sure that the organizing principle of the structure would limit what we might call the *play* of the structure. By orienting and organizing the coherence of the system, the center of a structure permits the play of its elements inside the total form. And even today the notion of a structure lacking any center represents the unthinkable itself. (1978b 278–79)

The most logical structure to "orient, balance, and organize" itself around a center is a circle. We may then assume that this image performs the function of the "icon" that Derrida says "is found on the back of the text and watches over it" (1987, 122).

The paradoxes involved with this image merge with Derrida's philosophical arguments and may indeed orient them. Moreover,

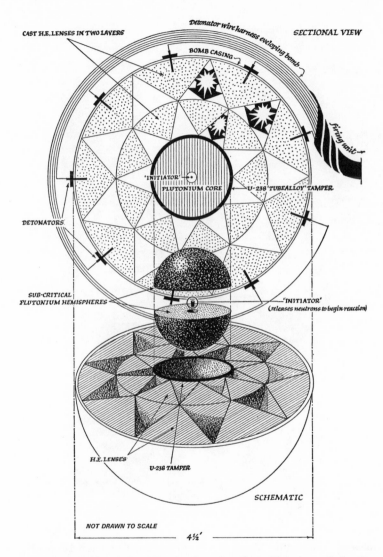

2 Bomb as Mandala. Illustration by Guy Fleming, from Lansing Lamont, *Day of Trinity* (New York: Atheneum, 1965), 176. Reprinted by permission of the author.

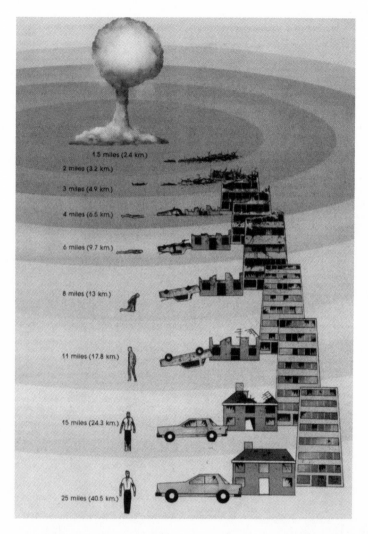

3 Circles of Destruction. From Christopher Chant and Ian Hogg, *Nuclear War in the 1980's?* (New York: Harper, 1983), 139. Copyright © 1983 by Nomad Publishers Ltd. Reprinted by permission of HarperCollins Publishers.

there is warranty for seeing the image in a nuclear version. Not only does Derrida suggest that a structure lacking a center represents the "unthinkable itself," but he also stresses the "play of [the] elements" within the structure—a play that, as we shall see, has certain affinities to fission and fusion—and later refers to "elements or atoms," implying the interchangeability of these terms (1978b, 281).

Finally, in the light of the foregoing analysis of zero it is worth noting that Derrida quotes Claude Lévi-Strauss's description of *mana* as "a zero symbolic value, that is to say, a sign marking the necessity of a symbolic content *supplementary* to that with which the signified is already loaded" (1978b, 290; Derrida's emphasis). This citation, as the italicized word stresses, reinforces Derrida's own argument that a center, lacking presence, is precisely that which must be supplemented. He goes on to quote Lévi-Strauss's note to this passage, containing a comparison of "zero symbolic value" to the linguistic notion of a "zero phoneme," which is something other than the simple absence of phonemes. Similarly, a concept like *mana*, Lévi-Strauss says, is "opposed to the absence of signification, without entailing by itself any particular signification." What Lévi-Strauss describes, in other words, is the presence of signification and the absence of a signified. It is exactly this curious status that characterizes zero in the history of mathematics. The version of zero that Derrida finds in Lévi-Strauss is likewise something other than a mere absence. A center that is *simply* absent would imply an alternative, its possible presence; and presence, Derrida argues, is an impossible dream. We must think instead of "the process of signification which orders the displacements and substitutions for this law of central presence—but a central presence which has never been itself, has always already been exiled from itself into its own substitute" (1978b, 280).

If this process is in some sense unthinkable, it is of that very unthinkability that Derrida encourages us to think. In what ways are we to think of it? The answer is represented by a move away from the center, from an originary concept whose ontological status we have discovered to be riddled with paradoxes. Instead of being grounded in a center our thoughts circle in an epistemological movement whose characteristic quality is that of *play.* Free play it may be—endless fission and fusion of ideas, substitution and supplementation, infinite extension in infinite process. But this infinitude is only possible through the evasion of structure, of that which would limit, select, and organize play. Structure opposes play and is opposed by it: "Play is the disruption of presence," Derrida says (1978b, 292)—but this does not mean that play is absence. Neither presence nor absence, play is movement, "the movement of supplementarity" (1978b, 289). In the context of Derrida's analysis of Lévi-Strauss, play would be related to *bricolage,* an art of combination in which what is combined are the discarded fragments of earlier discourses. Derrida claims that "every discourse is *bricoleur.* The engineer, whom Lévi-Strauss opposes to the *bricoleur,* should be the one to construct the totality of his language, syntax, and lexicon. . . . [He should be] the absolute origin of his own discourse" (1978b, 285). But Derrida argues that even the engineer is a myth, an origin myth. Since all myths, according to Lévi-Strauss, are *bricolage,* so are the engineer and the idea of origin. Lévi-Strauss admits that, though myths of origin may be found, one cannot find a myth that originates all other myths. Lacking that origin or center, the concept of structure collapses, leaving only *bricolage,* leaving only play.

2

What I am now doing is of course another act of *bricolage,* using the heterogeneous discourses I have been exploring so far: the nuclear circle around ground zero, the arithmetic paradoxes of the sign zero, and Derrida's deconstructive circle without a center. To these discourses I add another, Russell Hoban's post–nuclear-war novel, *Riddley Walker,* which is constructed and deconstructed around the same diagram as the others. This novel is, in more than one sense, exemplary: the insights to be gained from analyzing it illuminate the uneasy status of all literature written on the nuclear theme. For the attempt to write the unthinkable must always raise questions about what structure is adequate to this project, on what the structure grounds itself, and in what ways the writing moves.

Riddley Walker is about an hermeneutic activity rather like Lévi-Strauss's. Set in England two thousand years after a catastrophic nuclear war, the novel follows the efforts of its protagonists to return, in various ways, to that point of origin. The Pry Mincer wishes to recover the power of, if not the "1 Big 1," which is the nuclear bomb, then at least the "1 Littl 1," which is gunpowder. In short, he wants to restore the civilization that existed before the postwar "Bad Time." The aims of Riddley Walker are less clear, even to himself. But like the Pry Mincer he attempts to read the riddle of the "Eusa Story," the central myth of his society, in which we dimly recognize the account of a scientist's quest for the secret embodied in "the Littl Shynin Man the Addom" and of the price he pays for his success. In part, what dims our recognition (and in another way sharpens it) is the text's language, the conjectured speech of a devastated society. Quasi-illiterate, largely phonetic, it slows us to the pace of an oral culture, defamiliarizing the act of reading itself so that this process too becomes an unriddling.

Aside from the wide variety of its unriddlings, *Riddley Walker* follows an overall pattern typical of its genre: the traces of a long-past nuclear war are read—or misread—in an effort to decipher its nature. Often the act of reading these traces with a mythological mindset creates an origin that never existed. This happens, for instance, in Walter Miller's *A Canticle for Leibowitz,* where a grocery list and a circuit diagram belonging to an obscure scientist become objects of veneration charged with complex and mysterious significance. That transformation has a comic aspect, of course, but it is not necessarily being ridiculed. It teaches us something about mythologizing, a process not confined to "primitive" tribes. Spencer Weart shows how the bomb achieved mythological stature by being perceived in the mold of images that already existed. If we were to follow these images back in their turn we would not find an originary myth, any more than Lévi-Strauss has. Rather we would be likely to find, again, an activity of *reading back,* of inferring an origin from signs viewed as traces.

If *Riddley Walker* is then about the unriddling of myths, it is itself constructed like a myth. Knowledge that is hidden, possibly absent, and in any case unspeakable lies at the hypothetical center of a myth. It is thus to be found nowhere in the narrative—and everywhere. Though the knowledge is not spoken, it is nevertheless so important, so pervasive, that it must repeatedly appear in various guises. Principles of sameness and difference allow us to combine and separate motifs, images, the grammar of the story, until structures yield deep structures that manifest the knowledge of the problem the myth addresses, if not of the solution to that problem.

The heart of the myth that is *Riddley Walker* is "the idear of us." This is established in the first chapter by a conversation between the twelve-year-old Riddley and Lorna Elswint, "the oldes in our crowd," who are matter-of-factly revealed to be lovers. In the light of this essay's icon it is perhaps significant that what Lorna says comes as the two are lying together looking at the full moon, "all col and wite and oansome."

> Lorna said to me, "You know Riddley theres some thing in us it dont have no name."
> I said, "What thing is that?"
> She said, "Its some kynd of thing it aint us but yet its in us. Its looking out thru our eye hoals."

After some more talk, Lorna finishes with these words:

> "Now lissen what Im going to tel you Riddley. It thinks us but it dont think *like* us. It dont think the way we think. Plus like I said befor its afeart."

I said, "Whats it afeart of?"

She said, "Its afeart of being beartht."

I said, "How can that be? You said it ben here befor us. If it ben here all this time it musve ben beartht some time."

She said, "No it aint ben beartht it never does get beartht its all ways in the woom of things its all ways on the road."

Riddley identifies this moment as the origin of the story he is about to write:

Thats why I finely come to writing all this down. Thinking on what the idear of us myt be. Thinking on that thing whats in us lorn and loan and oansome. (1982, 6–7)

It is true that Lorna's words produce Riddley's journey in all its forms, including the narrative journey he now undertakes in writing down what has passed, in repeating the changes, in circling again the idea of us. If Lorna's words are an origin, though, it is evident that they cannot be *the origin*—as Riddley suggests just before he explains why he is writing:

Wel I cant say for cern no mor if I had any of them things in my mynd befor she tol me but ever since then it seams like they all ways ben there. Seams like I ben all ways thinking on that thing in us what thinks us but it dont think like us.

What is in question here is narrative itself, as well as "the idear of us"—and, most important, the relations between them. Riddley "cant say for cern no mor" which comes first. Such is the power of Lorna's "tel" that it challenges the assumption that an "idear of us" is at the origin, generating and grounding a narrative that always comes after. At the same time Riddley's comment helps us resist the notion that the idea of us is purely the production of narrative, for it seems as if the "some thing" Lorna describes has "all ways ben there." Yet in what sense is it there? Can we say that it is present in a presence? We may think on the thing that thinks us, that thinks the idea of us—but "it dont think like us." It is thus akin to Derrida's unthinkable, the absent center.

The best way of thinking about this problem is through Lorna's comment that what she is speaking of is "all ways in the woom of things its all ways on the road." The images seem to be appositive ways of figuring development or process, and yet there is contradiction between them as well. If we consider them in the overall context of the novel, we find them united in the icon of a circle around a zero. The zero here is ground zero, situated at Cambry, which used to be known as Canterbury before Bad Time; there, in a crypt of the vanished cathedral, is what Riddley calls the town's "woom." The circle of the womb is circled in its turn by the road passing through the dead towns around Cambry, which are listed in a children's rhyme called "Fools Circel 9wys." It is this circle that Riddley walks while unraveling his society's deepest myth and coming to some understanding of the idea of us.

Here walking itself is an emblem of continual process, of that which is always yet to be born, to be originated, to be present. "All ways on the road," walking has no beginning or determinable end.

> If the way is diffrent the end is diffrent. Becaws the end aint nothing only part of the way its jus that part of the way where you come to a stop. The end cud be any part of the way its in every step of the way thats why you bes go ballsy. (1982, 167)

In Derrida's analysis in *The Post Card,*

> the step or the *trans-* always already have the form of the return. It begins by coming back [*revenir*], by tending toward the annulling of its own process. This is also the progress of the proper which lets itself be enmeshed by this circular ring. Pleasure is found en route, the place of passage and moment of the ring. (1987, 397)

Derrida views the step as circular because it always comes back to itself; it exists only as repetition in process, each step simultaneously the same as the others and different from them.

Sameness and difference are represented in *Riddley Walker* by the "1" and the "2," whose relation is summed up by a line in the Eusa myth: "Lukin for the 1 yu wil aul ways fyn thay 2" (1982, 29). The 1 that is unity, presence, stability, splits continuously into difference, indeed into *différance*. The endless deferral, substitution, and movement that result are akin to play, and all the more so if in play 2s may in turn become 1s. Combination, that is, is another mode of the characteristic transformation, transition, of play. And since Derrida has already linked the *trans-* to the step, we may link play to the step as well. What Derrida calls "the play of repetition and the repetition of play" (1978b, 292) recalls the repetitive aspect of the step, its sameness. Yet its difference—its continuous moving out of an identity that it cannot possess (without ceasing to be, precisely, a step)—destines it not to any destination but rather to infinite change.

The Eusa myth speaks of change as simultaneously determining and determined by the idea of us. In the midst of the horrors of Bad Time, the Littl Shynin Man the Addom appears to Eusa and tells him "Yu let thay Nos. uv thay Master Chaynjis owt. Now yu mus go thru them aul" (1982, 33). But Eusa no longer knows the numbers or what it would mean to go through them. He asks:

Woan yu pleas tel me how menne Chaynjis thayr ar? The Littl Man sed, As menne as reqwyrd. Eusa sed, Reqwyrd by wut? The Littl Man sed, Reqwyrd by the idear uv yu. Eusa sed, Wut is the idear uv me? The Littl Man sed, That we doan no til yuv gon thru aul yur Chaynjis. (1982, 34)

The reasoning is circular here, and what it circles round is an absent center. Neither "thay Nos. uv thay Master Chaynjis" nor the "idear uv yu" can serve as origin of this circle or as its determining terminus. Only going through the changes of the circle can determine what is "reqwyrd."

The story of Riddley Walker depicts such a process of changes, gone through almost literally step by step in the "Fools Circel" of his journey. Riddley's loyalties shift among the various parties struggling for the power of a pre–nuclear-war knowledge. Affinities split: Riddley distances himself, first physically and then psychologically, from his "moon brother," the self-styled Ardship of Cambry. Enemies become friends: the Pry Mincer is brutal to Riddley at one moment and confiding the next; Riddley eventually takes him over, serving as his guide after the Pry Mincer is blinded by his second-in-command. Characters continually change and regroup according to the rubric of the 1 become 2, the 2 become 1.

Still closer to the open-ended spirit of play are the changes Riddley goes through in his thinking, a thinking that is always carried on through images. Often these images are the "elements or atoms" of an existent mythology. But a mythology may be dismantled and its pieces put together with others to form new structures—such is the spirit of *bricolage*—which themselves are apt to be dismantled and rebuilt. So Riddley combines images from his society's myths with images from his own journeying to create a private mythology that will serve his dual purpose: to follow through his changes step by step, and to understand the idea of us. In the end (which is also the step) the two are one, as we shall see.

An example of the changes that the novel rings on one image—changes that can be only briefly sketched here—is the play undergone by the "heart of the wood." In the first chapter this phrase applies to the heart shape that charcoal burners traditionally give to their smoldering piles. The origin of this custom is given in a story, not unrelated to myth, from Bad Time: a starving man and woman in a wood kill and eat their child, giving his heart to Mr. Clevver in exchange for fire, which then consumes them while they sleep beside it. In another myth, the Eusa story, the heart of the wood is found in the stone that is opened in the search for the atom. Within this mystic wood the Littl Shynin Man stands between the antlers of a "hart." The mystic wood is later literalized in the stone "wood" of the Gothic vault at Cambry, a vault that Riddley thinks of as both "woom" and heart, "meaning the veryes deap of it" (1982, 2). He then respells and reconceives the wood as "wud," as desire: "its the hart of the wanting to be" (1982, 160). And if he is referring to the origin of human desire, he conceives of it as something within us that, as Lorna would say, is not us. In a return to an earlier idea of the wood, this concept is imaged as a man's face with green vines and leaves growing out of its mouth. When Riddley encounters this image scrawled on a wall, he alters it, changing the branches into antlers and the long chin into the head of a stag, the Hart of the Wud. The face on the wall was that of the Pry Mincer; and the heart of his desires, the secret of gunpowder, is to be found with the charcoal burners, who have handed down in cryptic images the recipe for which they possess an essential ingredient.

The changes have come full circle, but this is not to say that they have come to rest. For thinking such changes creates in the one who thinks them a circularity that expands: "My head begun to feal like it were widening like circels on water I dint know if it wud ever stop I dint know where the end of it wud be" (1982, 116). That Riddley's image here is isomorphic with the diagram of nuclear explosion is not surprising, given the fission and fusion of changes like those just presented, and their relation to the Master Chaynjis of the atom. And the circle of Riddley's journey—mental as well as physical—is echoed in the circle of the Power Ring surrounding Cambry, a type of nuclear energy generator. The Ardship of Cambry tells Riddley, when they are trying to decide on their route, "If we go to Fork Stoan weare keaping the circel which thatwl be axel rating the Inner G you know. Thats what you do when you Power roun a ring. Which it looks like we bes ful that circel on a wyl yet" (1982, 86). This circling—this change and repetition, difference and sameness, fission and fusion—has an effect like that of the Power Ring: it produces the epistemological equivalent of an explosion.

But this explosion does not release knowledge—or, for that matter, power. What it creates is an awareness of absence—perhaps even, paradoxically, the awareness of an absence of awareness. Riddley comes to realize that "the onlyes power is no power"

(1982, 162). When he does so, he has passed through both versions of unriddling or "interpretation" described by Derrida:

> The one seeks to decipher, dreams of deciphering a truth or an origin which escapes play and the order of the sign, and which lives the necessity of interpretation as an exile. The other, which is no longer turned toward the origin, affirms play and tries to pass beyond man and humanism, the name of man being the name of that being who . . . has dreamed of full presence, the reassuring foundation, the origin and the end of play. (1978b, 292)

Yet Riddley's journey replaces that "name of man" with recognition of "something in us it dont have no name."

3

Speaking about what has no name, though, is another form of naming. How then are we to speak of the nameless? Riddley formulates the problem like this:

> Some times theres mor in the emty paper nor there is when you get the writing down on it. You try to word the big things and they tern ther backs on you. Yet youwl see stanning stoans and ther backs wil talk to you. The living stoan wil all ways have the living wood in it I know that. With the hart of the chyld in it which that hart of the chyld is in that same and very thing what lives inside us and afeart of being beartht. (1982, 156)

The argument here is, at first glance, a version of immanence. The "big things" turn their backs on you, as God did to Moses. Reading things from the back, without the knowledge that is "face to face," we can dimly detect what is at the core of their concentric, nested nature: within the stone is the wood, within the wood its heart, which is also the heart of the child and akin to the idea of us. Before we relinquish ourselves entirely to a pantheistic reading, though, we should remember that all this addresses the problem of words. It is words above all, as Derrida has reminded us, that exemplify knowledge gained from the back: "There is only the *back,* seen from the back, in what is written, such is the final word" (1987, 48). Yet Riddley indicates that these backs will talk to us, that there is a power within words. This power is linked to atomic power by the reference to "stanning stoans" that talk. The only stones that fit this description appear a few pages earlier, as Riddley enters Cambry: "When we come to the Ring Ditch the stannings of the Power Ring stood up wite agenst the dark like broakin teef" (1982, 150). The Power Ring may in fact be seen as an image of narrative. The power of narrative comes not from individual words, which will necessarily turn their backs on you in Derridean fashion. It comes from *motion,* motion that is circular, repetitive, and cumulative.

> Looking at them stannings I knowit inside me they musve had
> that 1 Big 1 going roun there regler. I cud feal the goast of it
> hy over me farring roun and out of site going roun that circel
> and coming back and roun agen EEEeeeeee. (1982, 150)

There is a "chemistery and fizzics" in which words may reach critical mass, generating a power that has nothing to do with attaining or finding the origin.

The Power Ring is isomorphic with another image in the book, the radar screen. When Riddley and the Ardship are trying to decide where to go next, Riddley has a flash of intuition:

> I had like a mynd flash of colourt lites with clicking and bleap-
> ing it wernt like nothing I ever acturely seen nor heard only in
> dreams. I cud like feal the woal circel of the dead towns in me
> and see a line of grean lite sweaping roun that circel from the
> senter.

Riddley describes to the Ardship what he is experiencing:

> "Its jus a line of grean lite sweaping and there come up blips."
> Which Id usit that word times a nuff but never til then did
> I ever think of putting the word *blip* to a blob of grean lite.
> (1982, 85)

Blip—along with other words such as *pirntowt*—has been carried over into Riddley's language from a lost technology. If a thing is *blipful* it is charged with a high degree of symbolic meaning—a meaning that is not arbitrary but that claims a peculiar connection to the energies within the thing. The "chemistery and fizzics" of those energies are revealed by a symbolic process that cannot be static. Motion is necessary, a movement through blips that are both the same and different and that accumulate to a point of revelation. The Ardship links the accumulative revelation of radar with the Power Ring, another version of the power of circular movement.

The circle, of course, need not inevitably be depicted as motion. The Greek geometers conceived of it as the static projection of points equidistant from a center. A radar screen creates a circle by pivoting a line segment around its fixed, static end. But it is a radically ungoverned idea of the circle that here represents narrative, and the "blip" of Riddley's narrative. In this notion a circle does not originate in a governing center but in a line that is continuously deflected from itself. This circle produces itself in a void, going through its changes without knowing how many of them there will have to be for it to return to itself, or even whether there will be a return to self. This is, one might say, a Derridean circle, produced step by step: through the circle of the step, continuously supplementing itself, it inscribes a larger hermeneutic circle round an absent center.

Any story is such a circle. Or that at least is the implication both of Riddley Walker's story and of what is said within it about stories. For instance, here is what Wayman Footling replies to Riddley's suggestion that Footling made up the story of how Hagmans Il got its name:

> That place Hagmans Il I use to wunner about it every time we come by it til finely that story come in to my head. That story cudnt come out of no where cud it so it musve come out of some where. Parbly it ben in that place from time back way back or may be in a nother place only the idear of it come to me there.

That dont make no odds. That storys jus what ever it is and
thats what storys are. (1982, 90)

In his own way, Footling is addressing the problem of origins.
His concluding "definition" of story echoes a passage in the Eusa
myth in which the Littl Shynin Man appears to Eusa during Bad
Time. The Pry Mincer describes this episode and comments on it
to Riddley:

> Whats that Littl Shyning Man say in *Eusa 26?* "Yu ar lukin at
> the idear uv me and I am it. Eusa sed, Wut is the idear uv yu?
> The Littl Man sed, It is wut it is." You see what I mean Riddley?
> *"It is wut it is."* Diffrent things at diffrent times may be. Its
> what ever it wants to be. (1982, 139)

In the full Eusa myth the statement emphasized by the Pry
Mincer is followed by another, of even greater pertinence to the
nature of story telling: "I aint the noing uv it Im onle jus the
showing uv it."

It is possible, then, to show something one does not know. This
is in fact what Riddley Walker's story does, and what Riddley will
continue to do after his story is over. For by the end of the book
he has begun putting on shows. Early on, he finds the blackened
figure of Punch in some diggings; when forced to display this to
the Pry Mincer, he discovers the unofficial existence of a complete
Punch and Judy show in mint condition. The subject of this show
is a primal violence in the idea of us, for Punch will always try to
kill his baby and a procession of other characters. The show falls
to Riddley after the Pry Mincer's death, and he begins to travel
with it around the circle of the towns, repeating the circle he has
made and will continue to make.

The puppet figure itself is an image of the unknowable idea of
us; it is as well an image of all the ways in which the unknowable
can be shown. At the puppet's center is an emptiness that is
perhaps more important than the puppeteer's hand. We cannot
name what is there any more than Lorna can: "Its some kynd of
thing it aint us but yet its in us. Its looking out thru our eye

hoals. . . . It thinks us but it dont think *like* us" (1982, 6–7). This connection accounts for Riddley's tranced interpretation of the puppet figure of Eusa, from the Pry Mincer's official show:

> I wernt acturely seeing Eusas head it wer jus *there* for me I
> cant say plainer nor that. Which it wunt stop getting bigger I
> cud smel the wood and the paint of it and the finger hoal so big
> it wer over all of us as big as the roof. Such a blackness. Not jus
> over us and all roun it wer coming up inside me as wel. Not jus
> wood and paint I smelt the blood and boan the redness in the
> black. The thot come to me: EUSAS HEAD IS DREAMING US.
> (1982, 58)

From all this it is impossible to say whether we are within the circle of that nameless thing, or whether it is at our center. The puppet, which promised a coherent allegory, has become paradoxical—as much so as the concept of the center itself. Derrida again:

> Classical thought concerning structure could say that the cen-
> ter is, paradoxically, *within* the structure and *outside it.* The
> center is at the center of the totality, and yet, since the center
> does not belong to the totality (is not part of the totality), the to-
> tality *has its center elsewhere.* The center is not the center.
> (1978b, 279)

Paradox, whatever its form, is a "showing" of unthinkableness. Unity is called into question, the 1 becomes 2, as when Eusa pulls apart the Littl Shynin Man:

> The Littl Man the Addom he begun tu cum a part he cryd, I wan
> tu go I wan tu stay. Eusa sed, Tel mor. The Addom sed, I wan tu
> dark I wan tu lyt I wan tu day I wan tu nyt. Eusa sed, Tel mor.
> The Addom sed, I wan tu woman I wan tu man. Eusa sed, Tel
> mor. The Addom sed, I wan tu plus I wan tu minus I wan tu big
> I wan tu littl I wan tu aul I wan tu nuthing. (1982, 30)

The paradoxes of the atom are also the paradoxes of the idea of us. Eusa, for instance, is defined as "the 1 what goes thru chaynjis. If hes chemistery or if hes a man" (1982, 139). And the same paradoxes must characterize that which *shows* the idea of us, whether it is narrative or puppetry.

"A figger show its got its oan chemistery and fizzics," Riddley says (1982, 199), underscoring the free play, the spontaneity, that is part of a Punch and Judy show. Spontaneity is also present in Lorna's first attempt to convey the thing that is in us:

> Say you get woak up suddn in the middl of the nite. 1 minim
> youre a sleap and the nex youre on your feet with a spear in
> your han. Wel it wernt you put that spear in your han it wer
> that other thing whats looking out thru your eye hoals.
> (1982, 6)

And this is perhaps the right moment to cite the author of *Riddley Walker,* who said in a 1984 interview, "Rationality is not enough to get us through what we have to get through" (Meyers 1984, 9). Something beyond knowing, that is, must be called upon if we are to come to terms with that which is called the unthinkable. It is "on us" to think about the unthinkable, with the help of anything that will show it. So Riddley, at the novel's end, thinks about his show: "Why is Punch crookit? Why wil he all ways kil the babby if he can? Parbly I wont never know its jus on me to think on it" (1982, 214). That we will "parbly never know" matters little. For it is in the *attempt* to think the unthinkable that the idea of us is formed, is enabled to go through its changes. That each of us can be thought of as "the 1 what goes thru chaynjis" is itself an idea of us, even if it is an idea without center, or origin, or presence.

What can narrative do, then, to help us through our changes? Showing without knowing, it indicates not an answer but a way: "Words in the air pirnt foot steps on the groun for us to put our feet in to" (1982, 116). Such has been the case with the children's rhyme "Fools Circel 9wys," which Riddley discovers that he has recapitulated not just in his geographical journey but in his psychological one. A journey is then the product of narrative, of many narratives. Words do not originate us, however, for Riddley is capable of reversing the sequence: "Walker is my name and I am the same. Riddley Walker. Walking my riddels where ever theyve took me and walking them now on this paper the same" (1982, 8).

Once again statements that circle around each other raise the question, Which produces which? Now, though, we may be more at home in these paradoxical circles. We find no point of rest; the ground beneath our feet is always ground zero; we circle that zero, "all ways on the road." That road is narrative as much as it is anything else: only by moving on it and being moved by it can we, despite not knowing, experience a continual showing.

> Which a show is some thing youre doing right now in this here time weare living in and youre doing the Chaynjis with Eusa.
> New things happening and new chances every time. (1982, 49)

Narrative can help us go through the changes required, step by step, word by word.

2 HOLOCAUST AND SACRIFICE

Hiroshima in the Morning

Early on the day he was to speak at the Johns Hopkins confer-
ence on structuralism, Jacques Lacan gazed from a Baltimore
hotel window and found the image of (in more senses than one)
his subject.

> It was not quite daylight and a neon sign indicated to me every
> minute the change of time, and naturally there was heavy traf-
> fic, and I remarked to myself that exactly all that I could see, ex-
> cept for some trees in the distance, was the result of thoughts,
> actively thinking thoughts where the function played by the
> subjects was not completely obvious. In any case the so-called
> *Dasein,* as a definition of the subject, was there in this rather
> intermittent or fading spectator. The best image to sum up the
> unconscious is Baltimore in the early morning. (1970, 189)

This image, assimilated into poststructural thought, surfaces in-
termittently in later work. Notably, Lacan's meditation was the
starting point for one of the first pieces of nuclear criticism, Dean
MacCannell's 1984 essay entitled "Baltimore in the Morning . . .
After: On the Forms of Post-Nuclear Leadership." Despite the
allusion to the 1983 made-for-TV movie, the essay is not about
the time after a future nuclear attack, but after a past one; and
the postnuclear leadership referred to is our own. Taking from
Lacan the notion that a culture can have an unconscious, Mac-

Cannell examines documents relating to the problem of the "inner city"—that is, to a certain social class inhabiting the city centers—and to the corresponding move of the educated and well-to-do into country and suburban towns. His conclusion is that, unconsciously of course, the United States is preparing to sacrifice its cities to nuclear attack, along with their socially problematic populations—thus rendering the enemy strikes relatively harmless or even beneficial. The argument is similar to that of Martha Bartter's later "Nuclear War as Urban Renewal" (1986). In the science fiction that Bartter studies, the annihilation of U.S. cities is followed by a return to the mythic wilderness of pastoral purification. Yet in all this talk of cities and nuclear war one city has been relegated to a place that one is tempted to call the unconscious. In Bartter's essay it appears not at all; in MacCannell's it occupies less than a page before the focus returns to contemporary urban concerns. And this liminal position is the one occupied in Western consciousness by that other city, city of the Other, Hiroshima.

1

Hiroshima in the morning, at 8:15 on the morning of August 6, 1945, cannot, like Baltimore, be described as an image of the unconscious. There is no such image; we are incapable of retaining one. In the words of a Hiroshima survivor, "Human emotions reach a point beyond which they cannot extend—something like a photographic process. If under certain conditions you expose a photographic plate to light, it becomes black; but if you continue to expose it, then it reaches a point where it turns white" (Lifton 1967, 33). Like the white shadows burnt into the sidewalks and walls of Hiroshima, we are only a blank, the mark of an absence, where the comprehension of that morning is concerned. This white mythology is admittedly an image, but only of our inability to image—an inability that all too easily shades over into denial, and the relegation of the whole city once more to the unconscious.

"Once more" I say because, on the basis of survivors' reports, there is warranty for describing what happened to Hiroshima as a massive irruption of the unconscious. "The flash that covered the city in morning mist," one survivor has written, "was much like an instant dream" (Lifton 1967, 34). In his study of atomic bomb survivors Robert Jay Lifton has noted the frequent use of such terms as "nightmare," "dream," and "dream realm" (1967, 34). For instance, Dr. Hachiya writes in his *Hiroshima Diary:*

> Outsiders . . . reported with amazement the spectacle of long files of people holding stolidly to a narrow, rough path when close by was a smooth easy road going in the same direction. The outsiders could not grasp the fact that they were witnessing the exodus of a people who walked in the realm of dreams. (1955, 54)

Many of those walkers later described their state at that time in a significant Japanese phrase: *muga-muchu,* "without self, without center" (Lifton 1967, 26). Externally, nothing remained of their old selves; clothing was stripped away, living bodies were swollen and burned beyond recognition. But more to the point, the instant after the blast the internal perception of its victims was that absolutely nothing remained of the reality around them, not even enough to orient them to the degree of its loss. "Hiroshima didn't exist," is all that one survivor can say; "Hiroshima just didn't exist" (Lifton 1967, 29). What people saw instead was so incomprehensible that it had to be assigned by them to a realm other than reality, the only realm in which such scenes could possibly have been experienced before, that of dream. The effects of shock upon its victims' perceptions contributed further to the dreamlike quality. Shock results in the deadening of pain and indeed of all physical sensation, a sense of unreality, a suspension of time or an effect of slow-motion, and the unfolding of events in silence. All of these characteristics are noted in survivors' accounts of their experience; more eerie than any other is the complete silence that fell over Hiroshima after the bomb, a silence so marked as to seem a palpable presence.

To link Hiroshima with the idea of a dream is not to deny the reality of what happened there, a reality that almost immediately after became manifest in material, inescapably corporeal ways that I will not describe. If I speak of a state of mind, it is because in this way alone is there some chance of a trajectory between our state and that of the people of Hiroshima. And this can occur only at the level of the unconscious—has in one sense already occurred. For if Hiroshima in the morning, after the bomb has fallen, is like a dream, one must ask whose dream it is. Who is the dreamer? The ready answer, of course, is that the dream is the unconscious creation of those who dropped the bomb; it is their unconscious. This is not an answer that can be easily dismissed. The long debate over the decision to drop the bomb, and the subsequent debate over that debate, include too many factors that cannot be accounted for by military strategy alone. Both Japanese and Americans have felt that race was probably a factor, making it easier for the enemy to fulfill its function of an Other on which could be projected all the qualities that a nation would wish to deny in itself. War ultimately aims at validating a national self, a national ego that, according to Elaine Scarry, aspires to "the dream that one will be . . . exempt from the condition of being embodied" (1985, 80). But this dream is only realized through the violently contrasting demonstration of the Other's embodiment. The Japanese were no less involved in this dynamic than were the Americans and no less committed to the validation of a consciously created national self.

This Japanese national self was represented and summed up by the cult of the emperor, a fact that might be suggestive to an analyst of dreams. In *The Interpretation of Dreams* Freud makes use of the Andersen tale of "The Emperor's New Clothes" in order to analyze the common dream of finding oneself naked in public. To the question of who the emperor might be Freud answers that he is the dreamer, stripped of the power of his conscious self. The

slow-moving automatons of Hiroshima, then—stripped of clothing, stripped of flesh, stripped of self—have been catapulted into
an unconscious that reverses their nation's consciously held
dream. They have been forced to live as reality the unmaking that
validates national making, and that is the price that war demands for it. The victims' experience, on both sides of any war, is
absorbed into the officially designated reality of the winner: the
consciousness of a certain national self, and the concept of history which supports it. As for the reality of the victims' unmaking, it is systematically relegated to the unconscious. This is
done by omitting it from language, or redescribing it, or margi-
nalizing it through metaphors that incorporate it into the sce-
nario of national making (Scarry 1985, 80).

It is through language, then, that war's aspect of unmaking is
removed from a nation's consciousness; it could consequently be
argued that language creates the unconscious to which it rele-
gates that aspect and which it thus conceals. And this may be so
not only after a war but during it, and "always already": we are
brought back to Lacan and his well-known dictum that the unconscious is structured as a language. In the Johns Hopkins
talk, Lacan warned his audience not to take this too literally: "I
have never said that the unconscious was an assembly of words,
but that the unconscious is precisely structured." In a sense the
dictum is a redundancy "because 'structured' and 'as a language'
for me mean exactly the same thing" (1970, 187–88). The meton-
ymy and metaphor that for Lacan together make up language
might just as well, he says, be the condensation and displacement
that for Freud make up dreams: the structuring principles are
the same in both versions of the unconscious. That structura-
tion—which is to say, that unconscious—is the Other to self in
Lacan's sense of the term: "The Other is the locus in which is
situated the chain of the signifier that governs whatever may be
made present of the subject—it is the field of that living being in
which the subject has to appear" (1979, 203). As is indicated by
the reference to "the chain of the signifier," the "field" here is

structured "as a language." It is a field that is far wider than the subject, which, when it appears, does so in an "intermittent" or "fading" way, like the lights of Baltimore emerging from the dimness of early morning. And while the Other is a locus or field that is all-encompassing, omnipresent, the subject has to make do with "whatever may be made present." Whatever may *not* be made present to the subject remains unconscious.

That morning at Hiroshima the "not present" manifested itself: "Hiroshima didn't exist." The city is made to feel the full force of the unconscious, the field within which the "fading" subject has to appear. In a blinding flash that field is revealed, inscribing itself on the bodies of Hiroshima's citizens. Some of those bodies it utterly consumes; some it brands forever with the sign of that moment, with the patterns of the kimonos worn then, with the angle of a body's posture, a face's tilt. We are then brought back to Scarry's basic concept: the body, guarantor of our own existence and the meaning of our world, becomes by its unmaking in torture or war the guarantor of another's meaning, discourse of an other—here of an Other that is a social unconscious. If that unconscious is structured as a language, we have some warranty for the dubious academicism of describing the bodies of Hiroshima's citizens as "inscribed" by the blast. Language, which is for Lacan equivalent to structure, is involved in this massive destructuring of the physical world; for all its abstractness it is as much the "cause" of the body's suffering at Hiroshima as is the physical fire.

Yet language, that ambiguous *pharmakon,* is remedy as well as poison. If language is structure, it can help us to make the world, to make something even of its unmaking on that August morning. And if the unconscious is structured as a language, it is language that may provide us with a road into the unconscious and with some understanding of it, as happens when we read the metonym and metaphor of dream.

The psychoanalytical process does not stop at dreams, of

course; Lacan heaps scorn on the formulation that *life is a dream:* "The real has to be sought beyond the dream—is what the dream has enveloped, hidden from us" (1979, 60). There is then a practical thrust to Lacanian psychoanalysis:

> What is a praxis? I doubt whether this term may be regarded as inappropriate to psycho-analysis. It is the broadest term to designate a concerted human action, whatever it may be, which places man in a position to treat the real by the symbolic. (1979, 6)

The links between language and Lacan's idea of the symbolic are well known; as for the problematic term of *the real,* I will refer only to one observation by Lacan:

> Is it not remarkable that, at the origin of the analytic experience, the real should have presented itself in the form of that which is *unassimilable* in it—in the form of the trauma, determining all that follows, and imposing on it an apparently accidental origin? (1979, 55)

The real to be treated here is that which is enveloped, hidden, in the dream that unexpectedly descended upon the citizens of Hiroshima. That "unassimilable" experience may be read in the classic terms of the trauma, magnified to overwhelming proportions. Indeed the bodies of Hiroshima's citizens often enact the deferral that is typical of trauma: years later, out of the body's unconscious, as it were, the trauma's effects come to the surface in the form of keloids and cancers—the scars of the unconscious, to borrow a Lacanian image, literalized and physically manifested. But the concept of deferral is not just a kind of determinism, an eternal return of the past in the present. It involves the revision of past events at a later date so that they fit in to a later phase of development or understanding. In a letter to Wilhelm Fliess (December 6, 1896) Freud refers to this process as a "retranscription," thus hinting at the agency of the letter in the unconscious, and at language's role in treating, in the form of the trauma, the real. Inscription, then, physical or psychical, may become transcription; scars of both kinds may be translated into new meanings; and the unconscious that is Hiroshima may emerge into a language that is adequate, if not to its impossible real, at least to us who are struggling to come to some kind of deferred terms with it.

2

This may take place; but has it? Has a language that is adequate to Hiroshima been found? Among the Japanese, where one would think the need is most urgent, the answer seems to be that it has not. As documented by John Whittier Treat, in his ongoing researches into Japanese A-bomb literature, the history of attempts to write Hiroshima is a history of failures. One of his essays may exemplify the overall pattern. "Hiroshima and the Place of the Narrator" (1989) deals with the work of Ōta Yōko, one of the best known of the Japanese atomic-bomb writers. "I live in a nation that has experienced the unprecedented," Ōta has stated; "I am unable to cling to the ordinary sorts of literature that we had before" (1989, 31). Yet her writing lapses helplessly into those ordinary sorts, though which sort she uses varies in the course of her career. As Treat reads her three major works, he detects in the sequence itself a significance, a trying-on of various solutions to a basic ambivalence:

> Her immediate project in authoring the most complete body of atomic-bomb literature we have today was devising the right calculus of mediated reception in her representation of Hiroshima: to preserve her status as a single author yet one of many victims and to preserve her readers' status as nonvictims made aware of the facts of Hiroshima but not of its ultimate significance for the survivors, for if that significance is ever to console it must remain restricted. (1989, 34)

Ōta's attempts to resolve this dilemma are represented more than anything else by the shifting place of the narrator in her work—the narrator being the point where communication itself is controlled. In *City of Corpses,* begun within a month after the bombing, the narrator is a stand-in for Ōta herself, and the testimonial form of the work excludes us from any participation other than a kind of voyeurism. Perhaps recognizing this, Ōta then turns to a "documentary novel," *Human Rags,* where the place of the narrator is diffused by an omniscient author among a number of points of view. The very fact that there is more than one implied narrator in Ōta's novel empowers the reader to choose between them, to judge. But this is to allow her *hibakusha* characters to be absorbed into a non*hibakusha* understanding, which necessarily diminishes their experience. This is the opposite extreme from the empowered but excluding voice of a single *hibakusha* testimonial, attempting to communicate even while insisting that communication of *this* is impossible. The third novel of this dialectic enacts not an *aufhebung* but a collapse of the problem in upon itself, and upon the writer. *Half-Human,* Treat says, is "very much about a writer trying to write" (1989, 43). Its protagonist, Oda, is again clearly a stand-in for the author. Yet by speaking of her now in the third person Ōta stands away from her stand-in. Everything about her is thrown into doubt, including her relation to the experience of the bombing. The result, Treat asserts, is "skeptical relations between readers and everyone else, including author, narrator and characters" (1989, 46). We see that what has been said of the narrator may apply as well to the reader, who occupies an equally uneasy place in atomic-bomb literature: the place of an understanding that is relinquished at our moral peril but that can never be achieved. "The right vantage point from which to view a holocaust is that of a corpse," says Jonathan Schell, "but from that vantage point, of course, there is nothing to report" (1982, 26).

Lacan might not be so sure of that. Nobody could accuse him of having nothing to report; but he characterizes the vantage point of an analyst precisely as that of a corpse:

The analyst intervenes concretely in the dialectic of analysis by pretending he is dead, by cadaverizing his position as the Chinese say, either by his silence when he is the Other with a capital *O,* or by annulling his own resistance when he is the other with a small *o.* In either case, and under the respective effects of the symbolic and the imaginary, he makes death present. (1977, 140)

This provocative statement suggests a way to attain a language "adequate" to Hiroshima that steps away from the question of who is proprietor—proprietor of communication itself as much as of the experience communicated. That experience I have described as an unprecedented manifestation of the Other, an Other that is by definition beyond proprietorship. Is it then also beyond language? Theoretically no, since it is structured as a language, structuring our selves in turn without our even knowing it. So we cannot discourse of the Other directly; it is precisely that which is excluded from our comprehension by the conscious self that emerges from that locus. At the same time it is always the Other of which we are discoursing, to the degree that "all discourse has its effect through the unconscious" (1977, 324). If we are to treat of/treat the real by the symbolic, then, this can only be done by going through the unconscious that envelops the real. We now see that the silence of the analyst, unlike the stunned silence of Hiroshima that day, has the purpose of a praxis: to allow for once the hearing of the subject's language, of its structuring force, of the Other in it which is akin to that Other revealed at Hiroshima.

The only language adequate to Hiroshima may then be the unconscious as it speaks in texts. Indeed, this may be the only language adequate to the Real of history in general, according to Fredric Jameson. He argues that

history is *not* a text, not a narrative, master or otherwise, but that, as an absent cause, it is inaccessible to us except in textual form, and that our approach to it and to the Real itself necessarily passes through its prior textualization, its narrativization in the political unconscious. (1981, 35)

Moreover, texts themselves may have an unconscious and may be—perhaps must be—interpreted accordingly. Jameson again:

Interpretation proper—what we have called "strong" rewriting, in distinction from the weak rewriting of ethical codes, which all in one way or another project various notions of the unity and coherence of consciousness—always presupposes, if not a conception of the unconscious itself, then at least some mechanism of mystification or repression in terms of which it would make sense to seek a latent meaning behind a manifest one, or to rewrite the surface categories of a text in the stronger language of a more fundamental interpretive code. (1981, 60)

The critic's writing is, or ought to be, a form of listening to the forces within the texts, rather like Freud's practice in *The Interpretation of Dreams*—in which, of course, he underscores the parallels between the work done by the dream and by literature. The praxis of treating the real by the symbolic may thus be accomplished by literary analysis as well as by psychoanalysis; the line between them is a permeable one.

It should be clear why I am now turning to a text that is ostensibly not about Hiroshima, a novel in which the bombing of that city is relegated to its usual place in Western literature, to the unconscious, here a textual unconscious. But I hope to show that such an unconscious is the real subject of the book, the Real enveloped within the dream that is *Gravity's Rainbow.*

3

Of the many reasons why Thomas Pynchon's novel encourages this sort of interpretation, not the least is the fact that *Gravity's Rainbow* begins with an actual dream. "A screaming comes across the sky" is the novel's first sentence; that screaming of an approaching rocket "holds," in an improbable temporal distortion, during the entire slow dream evacuation that follows—

holds that sequence within the arc of the descending rocket as the novel will later reveal itself to be similarly held. The sequence is extraordinarily rich in textures both physical and metaphysical. The dreamer has, this time, not missed the train that was Freud's symbol of death, and that now clinks along slowly in shadow, crowded with dim faces. There is no longer any escape possible: the evacuation of the city reveals itself "not as a disentanglement from, but a progressive *knotting into*" (1973, 3). The city is not only the target of the rocket but a symbol of the forces that produced it, and that inescapably produce its inhabitants. An enormous decrepit hotel is the journey's goal, shabby hell and microcosm of the city itself: "Underfoot crunches the oldest of city dirt, last crystallizations of all the city had denied, threatened, lied to its children" (1973, 4). And these words, with their evocation of the psychological under a geological or archeological figure, remind us that one of Freud's first figures for the unconscious in *Civilization and its Discontents* is the city of Rome.

Waking to another city, to London in the morning during the closing months of World War II, the dreamer, a U.S. soldier called "Pirate" Prentice, does not emerge into anything as comforting as "reality." The Chelsea maisonette that he and his friends are using as a barracks is a surreal scene, though its surrealism is perhaps less that of André Breton than of the Marx brothers. For instance, a "banana breakfast" of baroque exuberance goes far beyond mere credibility. And the dream lingers as well in Prentice's observation, from the roof, of a rocket in the far distance beginning its arc towards London. Thus, as Lacan has said, "The efficacy of the unconscious does not cease in the waking state" (1977, 163). Waking and dreaming worlds alike are produced by the unconscious—as they are in Pirate Prentice, gifted or cursed with the ability to experience the fantasies of others in his dreams and, later, outside them. One recalls Freud's observation, in *The Interpretation of Dreams:* "Real and imaginary events appear in dreams at first sight as of equal validity; and that is so not only in dreams but in the production of more important psychical structures" (1965, 323). This observation runs parallel to one made by Freud in his letter to Fliess (September 21, 1897) rejecting the seduction theory of hysteria: "There is no indication of reality in the unconscious, so that it is impossible to distinguish between truth and emotionally charged fiction" (Bonaparte, Freud, and Kris 1954, 215).

The language of *Gravity's Rainbow* also allies it to the unconscious and its dream work. Conventional narrative, when rendered in Pynchon's style, flickers with dense allusions, witticisms, restless verbal energies that seem on the verge of taking on lives of their own. And sometimes do take on lives of their own: in an early section the enigmatic phrase "You never did the Kenosha kid" is made to emerge with six different meanings out of six different scenarios. Language makes unpredictable sorties into the unconscious, challenging the view of language as controlled communication between an autonomous sender and receiver; one is tempted to draw a parallel to the challenge posed by Lacanian psychoanalysis to the mechanisms of American ego psychology. The language, moreover, is used to create an "emotionally charged fiction" that may in its turn become part of the unconscious, a discourse having its effect through the unconscious. *Gravity's Rainbow,* moving far beyond the historical research that underlies it, produces the feel of an unconscious, the unconscious of a whole time and culture.

In such ways the manifest content of Pynchon's novel may be read as that of a dream. Like a dream it has a latent content; and that latent content, I would argue, is summed up in Hiroshima. Though (with some notable exceptions) the time span of *Gravity's Rainbow* runs from December 1944 to September 1945, Hiroshima is all but absent. Aside from an ironic flicker when a Japanese speaks of returning to the peace of his hometown, the name of Hiroshima appears only once in the book, as a cryptic fragment:

In one of these streets, in the morning fog, plastered over two
slippery cobblestones, is a scrap of newspaper headline, with a
wirephoto of a giant white cock, dangling in the sky straight
downward out of a white pubic bush. The letters

MB DRO

ROSHI

appear above with the logo of some occupation newspaper, a
grinning glamour girl riding astraddle the cannon of a tank,
steel penis with slotted serpent head, 3rd Armored treads 'n'
triangle on a sweater rippling across her tits. The white image
has the same coherence, the hey-lookit-me smugness, as the
Cross does. It is not only a sudden white genital onset in the
sky—it is also, perhaps, a Tree. . . . (1973, 693–94)

The first thing we should note is that when Slothrop encounters
this scrap of paper he can have no idea of the content of the full
communiqué; nor can the paper give him any. For him, and momentarily for the reader, the scrap of paper is detached from the
realm of the factual; thereby both letter and image are rendered
cryptic. This cryptic quality, like that of dreams, encourages a
deciphering process that involves a spreading network of associations; within that net is captured more of the truth of Hiroshima than could have been presented by the full official page.
That truth is an unconscious one in two senses. It is a revelation
of the unconscious forces that manifest themselves at Hiroshima;
and it is a revelation that takes place, for Slothrop, only at the
unconscious level: "He doesn't remember sitting on the curb for
so long staring at the picture. But he did" (1973, 694).

And as for us, staring at another fragment, this fragment
from Pynchon's novel, what can we decipher of Hiroshima? Many
routes could be taken through the labyrinthine associations of
this passage; and I will be returning to it in a later chapter. At
this time, I will analyze only the genital pattern: the cloud from
the explosion is not a mushroom but "a giant white cock dangling in the sky straight downward out of a white pubic bush."
A simple identification of the bomb with phallic power does not

get us very far, explaining little about the nature of that power and the reasons for it to take the form that it did at Hiroshima. We get further if we approach the problem from the margins, literally. The official logo of the newspaper recapitulates the phallic element, situating it in such a way that it becomes highly charged psychologically. Moreover, the description of the logo bulks as large here as that of the wirephoto. It is thereby implied that "official," banal, and unthinkingly accepted patterns are linked with what was soon to become known as the Unthinkable; that there is a psychopathology of everyday life which eventually manifests itself in some such form as Hiroshima.

Beneath its cartoon sexuality, the logo is as disturbing an image as any analyzed by Freud: "a grinning glamour girl riding astraddle the cannon of a tank, steel penis." In terms of the castration complex, the woman has been given back that which the child originally perceived as having been taken away from her. The same image can be detected, again marginally, a little after the passage on which we are concentrating, in the narrator's description of Hiroshima on that morning: "At the instant it happened, the pale Virgin was rising in the east, head, shoulders, breasts, 17° 36' down to her maidenhead at the horizon." This curious deflection of interest onto a constellation seems to have only one purpose: to present the gigantic form of a woman, bit by bit, down to the genital area where something entirely unexpected is revealed, the phallic cloud depicted in the wirephoto. It remains ambiguous whether, "dangling in the sky straight downward," it is aimed at the virgin's maidenhead; or whether, rising from the horizon, the cloud restores to her the penis she was thought to lack. The same ambiguity is seen in the logo, where it is unclear whether the glamour girl is smugly flaunting "her" penis or enjoying the ride of her life on "his." In either case, directly or indirectly, the result is masculine empowerment. But the indirect route, the detour by way of the unconscious, takes a much more interesting form.

What is on the surface a grotesque image, calculated to terrify the male—that of a woman with a penis powerful as a steel cannon, explosive as a bomb—at another level brings to the male comfort and empowerment. For the classic castration complex depends on the apparent "evidence" that the threat of castration can be carried out, has been carried out on the female. It is this threat that gives its efficacy to the *Non du Père,* the "No!" by which the Father forbids the usurping of his sexual privileges. Now the evidence is reversed in order to deny the validity of that threat. And since the *no* of the Father, the *Non du Père,* is also the *Nom du Père,* the Name of the Father which is language, there are other consequences. The authority of language is denied, the chain of signifiers is broken, and the structured field which is our destiny is mastered—or so we hope. The sexual fantasy thus reveals itself to be the dream of full accession into the *Nom du Père,* into the power of the symbolic system.

Impossible as this dream may be, its consequences are real. The attempt to realize in the world something of which we are not even conscious leads ultimately to events such as Hiroshima. A fantasized revision of woman's body gives the power to inscribe on others' bodies a language from which one now feels oneself to be exempt. Indeed a hint of this can be detected in the logo, where we see the "3rd Armored treads 'n' triangle on a sweater rippling across her tits." This is partly, of course, proprietary confirmation of the phallic gaze, for whom the "hey-lookit-me smugness" is played out. But the tread marks are unsettling, evoking images of the 3rd Armored's tanks passing over the woman's body and so marking it. One recalls the somewhat sadistic ring of Lacan's language as he is describing the relation of the signified to the signifier: "The signifier has an active function in determining certain effects in which the signifiable appears as submitting to its mark, by becoming through that passion the signified" (1977, 284).

The overall terms of this analysis are reinforced by their appearance throughout *Gravity's Rainbow.* There is, after all, an actual scene of castration in the novel. Though it misfires because of a case of mistaken identity, it is meant for Tyrone Slothrop. Its purpose is to undo the unique properties of Slothrop's penis, properties that were acquired by a process of Pavlovian conditioning in early childhood. His father in effect sold him to a psychologist working for the state; he now has an erection at any locale that will shortly be hit by a rocket. This affinity may be in part due to a fact that links the mechanistic nature of Pavlovian psychology to the larger mechanisms of World War II: the psychologist who conducted the experiments upon young Tyrone was also the developer of Imipolex G, a plastic used in German rocketry. Slothrop's penis is then a curiously literal version of the phallus as signifier, "the signifier intended to designate as a whole the effects of the signified, in that the signifier conditions them by its presence as a signifier" (Lacan 1977, 285). The reference to conditioning here allows us to distinguish Slothrop's flesh-and-blood penis, which has been conditioned, from a very different version of conditioning signified by the (conceptual) phallus. If we ask who is responsible for that conditioning we must go beyond the psychologist, beyond the father to the Father that is the entire structuring system within which (as he gradually discovers) Slothrop is bound. Searching for the secret of his childhood trauma, Slothrop finds only a widening network of connections on all levels of society, where even supposed enemies are knotted together in vast cartels. What he learns on a social level is the Lacanian truth of "his relation as a subject to the signifier" (1977, 287).

Not surprisingly, Slothrop's reaction to all this is full-blown paranoia, a common effect of the castration complex. Paranoia may arise from a specific and personal trauma (such as being sold by your father and having your penis experimented upon); but it may also arise from the general nature of the human situation itself. To begin with, we must resist the tendency (a somewhat paranoid one) to make the simple distinction between "us" and "them," as Slothrop generally makes it, between the paranoid and the aggressor. Paranoia and aggressivity are recognized by psychoanalysis as two sides of the same coin. So the paranoid vision repeatedly referred to in *Gravity's Rainbow* when turned inside out is a study of aggression. In Lacanian terms, it is the inversion of the aggressivity that arises out of the futile and continually frustrated attempt at full realization of the self—first in the imaginary stage, and later through the symbolic system. We are dealing then with "a correlative tension of the narcissistic structure in the coming-into-being (*devenir*) of the subject" (1977, 22). Not a personal trauma but a universal condition is the source of paranoid aggressivity. Its recurrent expression on the national scale is war, which Lacan ironically describes as "the inevitable and necessary midwife of all progress in our organization" (1977, 27). There is of course no such progress—not even, for the most part, in the understanding of war's nature. To link war to the castration complex, as I have done above; to read it as a signifying act, as the fantasy of full accession into the signifying system, as the subject *becoming* the signifier (no longer subject to the signifier) if only for an other—these notions, no doubt, will seem bizarre to some. As is necessarily the case for the contents of an unconscious, before they manifest themselves through material symptoms in the world.

The ways in which latent content is manifested in *Gravity's Rainbow* are the classic ones of displacement and condensation. In a novel written during the nuclear age, the view of German rocketry as the ultimate in terror can only be ironic; it is clearly the displacement of a threat that is so much more terrifying than that one that it cannot be apprehended directly. Moreover, as Slothrop attempts to obtain a direct understanding of the mysterious 00000 rocket, indirections proliferate. One clue leads to another; Ariadne's thread becomes itself the labyrinth. The process is metonymic, with parts substituting for wholes and for the wholeness of understanding toward which Slothrop aspires. Finally the wholeness of his own self is lost as he splinters into a series of momentary identities. This is parallel to a movement in the novel which expands characters, alliances, cartels, until the sheer multiplied mass of these begins to fall back on itself in a process akin to condensation. Not that we are ever able to sum up their underlying relations, the plot that the paranoid is sure exists out there. The process of which I am speaking takes place in the reader's perception, at a time determined by the reader's own rhythms; and it takes place at the level of the unconscious. If condensation is a metaphor, it remains impossible to say exactly what this novel is a metaphor *of*. I have suggested Hiroshima; but perhaps it is Hiroshima that is the metaphor, condensation of all the forces that can only be sensed through their effects.

The "resolution" of *Gravity's Rainbow* is thus nobody's property: it is always that of the Other. The "suspense" that is resolved is equally hard to pin down, and all the more so for being literal. In the first sentence of the novel "a screaming comes across the sky" as a rocket approaches; in the last pages of *Gravity's Rainbow* a rocket descends. The rocket's arc, like a perverse rainbow, thus holds all the novel's events in suspense—a suspense that is simultaneously literary, psychological, political. Literary: the search for a secret, as in the detective novel, whose hero may uncover (in Ross MacDonald's Los Angeles, for instance) a pattern of expanding corruption similar to that which in *Gravity's Rainbow* extends from the city to the world, leaving no detached Archimedean point from which the secret can be observed. Psychological: deferral, where the secret may not even be recognized as such until some time later and is meanwhile relegated to that deepest locus of secrecy, the unconscious. Political: nuclear politics as another case of continued deferral. Of all the horrors of Hiroshima, that which distinguishes it from every comparable horror is that it is *not finished.* I am speaking of the deferred action of the bomb not on the bodies of its victims but on the minds of all those who live in the world that it dominates. Robert Maniquis (1983) has explicated the ways in which we are held hostage by the bomb, whose terrorism disposes us against the taking of risks and encourages us to become malleable citizens. However, the deepest ways in which we are hostages remain secret, as it is impossible for us to face them. We relegate the implications of Hiroshima to the unconscious and suspend them there.

It is then at the level of the unconscious that we must first seek a resolution of the nuclear dilemma, a freeing from the paralysis that suspends our ability to act. And it is through the agency of the letter in the unconscious that this may be done, as books like *Gravity's Rainbow* demonstrate. Literary, psychological, and political are woven together in an intricate complex situated in the unconscious, "the field . . . in which the subject has to appear." For the most part that field, and our place in it, remains unknown and unknowable by us. But the truth of its existence may sometimes descend upon us like an instant dream that embodies itself in the world, as it did on August 6, 1945.

Whether Pynchon intended all this, whether he is a Lacanian or even a Freudian—these questions are beside the point. If Lacan's theories partake of truth—a word that he insists on—then they must be "there" in that presence that is defined by its absence from consciousness. And a writer's associations may then coalesce in language that hints at that other language, language of the Other, which is the unconscious. Hints are what emerge, effects at the level of the unconscious, as we look at a certain fragmentary communiqué, and look at Slothrop looking at it. Our perception, like his, is a dim one; the entire encounter takes place, after all, in "morning fog." Only, as "the fog whitens into morning" while Slothrop watches the ambiguous image of the white cloud, we sense a significance to this reiterated whiteness: the cloud that is the sign of Hiroshima is akin to the one that envelops him. The forces that manifested themselves at Hiroshima are latent in our lives. Attempting to read the unconscious through a contained text, we remain oblivious of the degree to which it continues beyond its borders, containing us in turn.

Yet momentary and cryptic flashes of insight punctuate the dimness of our apprehension, like the flickering of traffic in Baltimore's faint dawn. And these we must learn to read, for all the reasons I have stressed in this tale of two cities, which indeed are one. Hiroshima's terrible difference from Baltimore is the product of a common structuring dynamic that contains them both. And what Hiroshima was, Baltimore may yet become . . . the morning after.

The Sacrificial Text

I was a bit more than four years old, my parents were down in the garden, I was alone with her in what we used to call the veranda. She was sleeping in her cradle, I remember only the celluloid baby doll that was aflame in two seconds, nothing else (neither having lit it myself, nor the slightest emotion today, only my parents running up).

So Jacques Derrida, or a persona going by that name, recalls in *The Post Card* an incident from his childhood. A little later he sums it up in an unexpected way: "Doubtless," he says, "this was the first desired holocaust" (1987, 253–54).

If the first desired holocaust is this instance of sibling rivalry, the last is the nuclear holocaust that eats away at so many pages of *The Post Card*. Frances Ferguson has argued that part of the appeal of the "nuclear sublime" is that it will disencumber us from the existence of other people, which "seems like an accident that has befallen us" (1984, 9). On a global scale, then, it satisfies the claims of the same infantile ego that Derrida has described. But in the context of *The Post Card* the appeal of the last holocaust is that it will consume the archive that makes possible the letters of the "Envois," belles lettres, literature itself. In fact, nuclear fire will meet a corresponding element within literature. Just as Derrida characterizes nuclear war as "fabulously textual," through and through," so he claims that "literature has always belonged to the nuclear epoch" (1984, 23, 27). This is so to the degree that literature and nuclear holocaust share "the historical and ahistorical horizon of an absolute self-destructibility without apocalypse, without revelation of its own truth, without absolute knowledge." The "unassimilable wholly other" of nuclear holocaust, as Derrida calls it, is akin to the otherness that lies both beyond and within any text. What is desired, then, is an ultimate deconstruction.

Yet the anecdote of the celluloid doll, while expressing this desire, offers an alternative to it. For what is enacted here is a substitution: violence is deflected from the baby sister through a mimetic representation. For it is specifically a "baby" doll that is burned, in place of the baby in the cradle. Two overlapping points suggest themselves here. First, the substitution, the deflecting of violence from its real aim and onto a "safe" victim, means that the process described here is analogous to that of sacrifice; the holocaust, whatever the form in which it is ultimately desired, in its first form is a burnt offering of the most ancient kind. Second, the fact that it is an *imitation* of the child which is burned invites us to reconsider mimesis in general, and literary mimesis in particular. Through such a consideration I hope to indicate a role for literature in relation to nuclear holocaust that is other than that of an archive doomed to be destroyed by all that lies beyond the power of the letter, like the library of Umberto Eco's monastery. Written pages may yield more than fuel for the holocaust if they are willing to sacrifice themselves, to perform a sacrificial function.

1

On the nature of sacrifice, it is René Girard who has provided the key concepts. In *Violence and the Sacred* he argues that the historical moment of sacrifice marks the transition from the animal to the human, defined in terms of such ordering structures as language and social institutions. Sacrifice is the necessary resolution of a primordial violence that would otherwise be as uncontained as it is inevitable. That inevitability of violence is explained by Girard's theory of "mimetic desire." According to this, the self is formed through identification with others, models that it imitates; and this imitation includes the desires of those others. Desire, in Girard's view, is only secondarily desire of the object; primarily it is the desire of the other, that which the other has taught the self to desire. Having learnt its lesson well, the self imitates that desire, with unforeseen consequences: "When any gesture of appropriation is imitated, it simply means that two hands will reach for the same object simultaneously: conflict cannot fail to result" (Girard 1978, 201). The self is in a double bind like that delineated by Gregory Bateson, where the child is told, "Be like me" and then—in the areas of power and sexuality, for instance—is told, "Do not be like me." The mimesis that should ensure the cohesion of the family, or of the community, thus instead results in conflict.

The violence of such conflict poses the gravest threat to a primitive community, for it engenders a further mimesis of its own, a reciprocity without end. Vengeance spreads the contagion of violence ever wider; those who attempt to intervene find their attempts greeted with hostility and in turn are soon drawn into the conflict. Everyone wishes to speak the final word on violence, or to enact it. But in consequence the scope of violence only widens, until the entire community is threatened. Finally, its tensions discover, spontaneously, a solution. Possessed by the frenzy of a mob—frenzy that will later be seen as sacred—the community falls upon an arbitrary victim, whose only qualifications are to be vulnerable and close at hand, and destroys him. He is killed by all for the sake of all, for the sake of the endangered society. Not that this is thought through at the moment of frenzied mob action. The mob seeks only the release of its own tense trajectory towards violence. Not until afterwards is it apparent that all are purged, just as all are guilty. Because all are guilty, no revenge is taken. The escalating sequence of violence is broken, and the community is bound together by blood.

This resolution of an already existing violence, spontaneously discovered by the community, is commemorated and imitated later—but the sacrifice now comes *before* violence and is meant to prevent it. The original spontaneously chosen victim, himself a surrogate for the imperiled community, is replaced by another victim who substitutes for him in a ritual sacrifice. Ancient Athens, for instance, would choose a ritual victim from among a number of people designated for that purpose and maintained at public expense. Whenever a potential calamity threatened the community, a *pharmakos,* as he was called, was sacrificed. Derrida has made much of the fact that the word *pharmakos,* applied to rhetoric in the *Phaedrus,* means both "poison" and "remedy": this is less of a contradiction when we remember the scapegoat mechanism, in which a victim is made to bear all the evils that infect the community but through his sacrifice heals it, purging it of those evils. The *pharmakos* could also be designated a *katharma,* the Greek term for an evil object extracted by means of a ritual, and related to the medical *katharsis* or "purging"— which in turn is used by Aristotle, of course, to describe the effects of tragedy.

Tragedy, in Girard's view, is often an implicit comment on the origin of sacrificial rites, and on the price that must be paid to ensure the community's survival. Girard analyzes *Oedipus Rex,* for instance, in terms of a conflictual seesaw that ultimately finds its scapegoat in Oedipus himself. The poison having been expelled from plague-ridden Thebes, it is recognized as a precious medicine in *Oedipus at Colonnus,* where the only conflict is over who shall be allowed to venerate the victim most. Tragedy thus validates the institution of ritual sacrifice—but it also threatens it, because it comes dangerously close to revealing the secret of its arbitrary origins, and to questioning the careful distinction between "impure" and "pure" (i.e., sacrificial) violence. Yet tragedy is itself a ritual—or rather the mimesis of a ritual which is again the mimesis of an original spontaneous sacrifice—and for that reason produces the desired catharsis.

Girard's theory is here applied to literature, explicating it as something that looks back to a preexistent event upon which its own existence is based. Yet literature is not a latecomer but is linked to the theory throughout. This link emerges more strongly if we juxtapose Girard's ideas with those of Jacques Lacan, for whom the matrix of one's existence is always already literary. The result is a certain conflict between the two (and therefore a certain violence). This may be expressed in terms of what Girard calls "the sacred difference that each faction strives to wrest from the other" (1977, 205). That sacred difference centers on the concept of mimesis.

It is Lacan's mirror stage that raises the most issues for any theory of mimesis. In this stage the child, for the first time, grasps the idea of a totalized self through the recognition of its mirror image. Lacan comments in the following densely packed sentence:

> This jubilant assumption of his specular image by the child at the *infans* stage . . . would seem to exhibit in an exemplary situation the symbolic matrix in which the *I* is precipitated in a primordial form, before it is objectified in the dialectic of identification with the other, and before language restores to it, in the universal, its function as subject. (1977, 2)

We actually have three stages of mimesis here, of which the last is the most explicitly literary. The first is the mirror stage itself, named for an incident that, it is important to note, is an "exemplary situation" that "would seem to exhibit" the workings of Lacan's theory. While that theory makes universal claims, the situation does not. What, for instance, performs the functions of the mirror in places and times where the mirror does not exist? Pools of water, polished brass, are somewhat beside the point. We must rather move to the moment after the mirror stage, characterized by "the dialectic of identification with the other." Girard's version of this is comprehensive enough that it can assume the main functions of the mirror stage:

> Once his basic needs are satisfied (indeed, sometimes even before), man is subject to intense desires, though he may not know precisely for what. The reason is that he desires being, something he himself lacks and which some other person seems to possess. The subject thus looks to that other person to inform him of what he should desire in order to acquire that being. If the model, who is apparently already endowed with superior being, desires some object, that object must surely be capable of conferring an even greater plenitude of being. (1977, 146)

The plenitude of being here is not that conveyed by the specular image, but by the image of the other. This image, though it is less directly recognizable as the "Ideal-I," nevertheless has all the pertinent qualities Lacan claims for the specular one: "The total form of the body by which the subject anticipates as in a mirage the maturation of his power is given to him only as a Gestalt, that is to say, in an exteriority in which this form is certainly more constituent than constituted . . . in contrast with the turbulent movements that the subject feels are animating him" (1977, 2). The assumption of his image by the child is "jubilant," then, because it seems to satisfy an already existent desire for the autonomy of being which he has perceived others to have and himself to lack.

But if I am allowing Girard's version of mimesis to overwrite Lacan's here, there is still much that Girard may learn from Lacan. Girard makes a sweeping claim that the spontaneous moment of sacrifice, because it "discovers" the symbolic, is the birth of language and marks the transition from animal to human. This claim ignores all the symbolic systems that might precede this one; that precede even the human, as shown in studies of animal societies; and that certainly precede the individual subject.

It is into this symbolic system that the "I" is now precipitated; and that system holds out the false promise of realizing the image of the totalized self which the child has glimpsed in the mirror. But instead, language merely alienates the subject further. It intensifies the subject's rupture from the real, moving it along an endless chain of signifiers toward an unattainable end represented by an image on the other side of a glass. Yet this rupture may also be restorative, may restore to the subject something of what was lost in the search for a static, completed ego-ideal. How language may accomplish this in the subject will be clearer if we first see how it accomplishes this in a text.

2

Bernard Malamud's last novel, *God's Grace,* deals with questions of mimesis; of language; of the distinctions between the human and the inhuman, both animal and divine; and with the relation of all of these to the nuclear dilemma. The book begins with one of the most remarkable opening sentences I know: "This is that story." The implication is that the story we are about to hear is so familiar to us that it need not be specifically designated; it is the one we have always already been living with. What follows the sentence is a description of nuclear aftermath:

The heaving high seas were laden with scum
The dull sky glowed red
Dust and ashes drifted in the wind circling the earth
The burdened seas slanted this way, and that, flooding the
  scorched land under a daylight moon
A black oily rain rained
No one was there

The implication of the opening sentence, then, is that nuclear holocaust is already familiar to us and has been played out in our unconscious countless times. It is the repressed that eternally returns, in unexpected ways and various guises. Moreover, nuclear holocaust's "fabulously textual" nature here becomes literally one story among others. It is thus situated in a chain of differing and deferring stories; for when Calvin Cohn, the book's protagonist, considers the question of where stories come from, he can only say that they come "from other stories" (1982, 70). In a sense, then, "this" story is always "that" story; there is always a story before the story. This is true of *God's Grace* itself, which is among other things a Robinsonade; *Romeo and Juliet* replayed by Calvin Cohn and a female chimpanzee named Mary Madelyn; the story of Abraham and Isaac; and Jane Goodall's book on monkeys.

That stories imitate other stories is the first in a series of variations on the theme of mimesis. According to Cohn it is not only stories that imitate other stories; so do we. "He thought that the story one heard most probably became the one he would live out" (1982, 85). And we in turn desire to be imitated. In Cohn's case, there are no other humans he could desire to imitate him. God, speaking out of the customary cloud, has assured him that he is the only human survivor, a divine oversight that is to be remedied in the near future. Sheltered in a small submersible observing the ocean floor at the moment the cataclysm struck, Cohn has ascended to his oceanographic research vessel to find it deserted except for a small chimp named Buz, the pet of one of his fellow scientists. After they are cast ashore on an island, other monkeys gradually appear. "Monkey see, monkey do": mimesis offers the opportunity for a creative evolution, Cohn thinks. He sets about trying to make the monkeys more human, according to his definition of the human, a definition that humans themselves have not lived up to:

> Cohn said he thought to be human was to be responsible to
> and protective of life and civilization.
> Buz said he would rather be a chimp. (1982, 70)

The fact that Buz can talk is accounted for by his previous owner's desire to make him more human. Under a frayed bandage around the monkey's neck, Cohn finds a scar with two wires protruding from it: when the wires are joined, Buz is able to speak through an artificial larynx. He is consequently able to teach the other monkeys on the island to imitate his speech.

Cohn too enacts a mimesis—though it is an unconscious one, revealed mostly by physical changes. His bowed legs, increasingly suffering from lack of calcium, make him somewhat monkeylike. But by the time God calls in his last outstanding debt Cohn has acquired a long white beard and the look of a patriarch, perhaps even the look conventionally assigned to God himself. The role that Cohn plays out is, in many versions, that of the Father.

Buz learns to call Cohn "Dad" and is raised by him through his chimpanzee adolescence to maturity. Their relationship is characterized by the mimetic double bind. Underlying Cohn's teachings is the implicit message "Be like me—but only up to a point." That point is the classical site of the Oedipus complex. Buz's burgeoning sexuality seeks an outlet, but there is only one female chimpanzee on the island, the one named Mary Madelyn. Sensitive, romantic, aspiring to higher things, she is in love with Calvin Cohn. Eventually, Cohn mates with her in an attempt to produce offspring that will speed up the evolutionary clock. This attempt is successful, but it also produces a smoldering sexual resentment that triggers the final cataclysm of violence on the island. All this is in keeping with Girard's theories of the mimetic sequence as it is played out in father and son.

Cohn is also Father to a wider family, that of the full community of monkeys. Bringer of civilization, teacher, he finally becomes lawgiver as well. To be sure, he softens the terminology; he promulgates not ten commandments but seven Admonitions, modest and nonauthoritarian. For example, number six: "Altruism is possible, if not probable. Keep trying." The Admonitions are baked in clay and affixed to the face of a cliff. For all their modesty, they set out the Law; and Cohn their author is the Father who is Law, the Father as Law.

The Law is made up of words, and words are an important part of Cohn's mimesis. Cohn himself has suggested that he, like all of us, is the mimesis of a story. However, it will be unclear which story he is living out until it is determined which story he has heard most often, though undoubtedly in various guises. Those guises may be less various than they seem, stories less different from one another than they appear. For if stories come from other stories, as Cohn has told Buz, we may ask with Buz where those stories come from in their turn. Here is Cohn's answer:

> "Somebody spoke a metaphor and that broke into a story. Man began to tell them to keep his life from washing away."
>
> "Which was the first story?"
>
> "God inventing himself."
>
> "How did he do thot?" [*sic:* Buz has an accent, the mimetic trace of his first, German owner.]
>
> "He began, He's the God of Beginnings. He said the word and the earth began. If you tell stories you can say what God's doing." (1982, 70)

As Cohn sees him, God is an author in the literary sense: Author of the universe, he is a connoisseur of stories and plays them out in human lives. Sometimes the stories are not very well constructed. Sometimes we don't understand them very well. All that Cohn can understand is that "God was Torah. He was made of words" (1982, 92). Lacan, approaching the subject differently, comes to a similar conclusion: "That the symbolic is the support of that which was made into God, is beyond doubt" (1985, 154). But all else about God is thrown into doubt by the speech that is his means of manifestation. In Seminar III Lacan plays on God's statement "I am who I am." The Hebrew "I am," *Jaweh,* is Jehovah, the name of the Father. In the French, however, "Je suis celui qui suis" allows us to hear an alternate meaning: "I am he who follows." Apart from the implications of that meaning, the fact of the multiple meanings is itself significant. The instability of language—which is yet the "support" of the concept of God—

is present in any language, undermining God's presence or pre-
sentness. In Cohn's mimeticism, he follows God's nature through
words: telling stories, teaching, attempting to author a new
world in his monkey-populated island. The failure of his attempts
is the failure of words.

The final cataclysmic violence on Cohn's island is signaled by
the loss of speech, by the monkeys' regression to their earlier
modes. Before they had learned to speak, violence was often substituted for the words that would not come: for instance, a somewhat backward gorilla named George overturns a seder table
when he is unable to make an after-dinner speech. All this seems
to indicate that words and violence are a binary opposition, with
each displacing the other. However, it may be argued that the
passage to words itself has a violent aspect, and it has been so
argued by Lacan: "Psychoanalysts showed that there were symptoms without any cause other than this: that the human is
afflicted, if I may say so, with language. . . . What is social," he
continues, "is always a wound" (*Scilicet* 6/7, 17; quoted in
MacCannell 1986, 46). And insofar as the symbolic system
subsumes both the social and the linguistic, language is a wound
that never closes. The moment of taking upon oneself the Name
of the Father is then designated by the term *coupure* or "cut."
This figure of speech is literalized repeatedly in Malamud's novel,
and always in ways that link it to language. Buz's first father
has given him speech by implanting an artificial larynx in an
operation that is literally a throat cutting. When Buz rebels
against his second father, Cohn punishes him by cutting the exposed wires that were joined to give him speech. And when the
son, mute and violent, overthrows the father, he does so by cutting his throat. This ends Cohn's life and the words that make up
his story.

That story turns out, in the end, to be one of the stories that
Cohn told Buz, the story of Abraham and Isaac. In the last scene
of the novel, it is enacted in recognizably biblical form. The
sacrificial party ascends a mountain; the victim carries a bundle

of sticks for the burnt offering that is to be himself; a rude altar is the journey's goal. But it is a monkey who leads a man to the sacrifice; a son who sacrifices his father; and no angel appears to substitute a goat at the last moment. "This is that story," then, not in the sense of a simple equation between the two. Their identity and their difference are apprehended simultaneously. Moreover, this story is embedded in the longer story of *God's Grace* and derives the significance of its difference from its relation to it. *Coupure,* in that longer story, created the order of words which is associated with the father. Now the Father, the one who follows, is led to the sacrifice in a series of stacked associations. Cohn is both familial father and, mimetically, heavenly Father. As God he is story, he is "made of words"; thus Cohn is the "Name-of-the-Father." And this, it seems, is what is sacrificed.

Yet what Lacan calls the "Name-of-the-Father" will not be disposed of by killing someone who goes by that name—as Malamud himself seems to indicate. Cohn comes to represent all the things that he wishes to eliminate in the new world he has a chance to author. A decent, well-intentioned man who abhors violence, he has no desire to be God's stand-in; and his mimesis is involuntary. At the moment of Cohn's death we see that another significant mimesis has taken place. George, the ape who overturned the seder table, has been listening all along to a windup phonograph playing records of Cohn's father, a cantor, but to no apparent effect. Now we see, suddenly, that he has achieved a breakthrough:

> In a tall tree in the valley below, George the gorilla, wearing a mud-stained white yarmulke he had one day found in the woods, chanted, "Sh'ma, Yisroel, the Lord our God is one."
> (1982, 223)

The ape represents the continual re-presentation of Father, Law, and Word—more precisely "chant" here, I suppose—and all of these are "one." There is no escape.

Civilization seems to have come to an end, as the island's apocalypse recapitulates in miniature the global one. In another sense civilization continues beyond this violence, as George assumes the patriarchal role. The sense in which it continues is that in which it is itself violent, enacts a violence upon its members. Built upon the figurative violence of the *coupure,* it finds its ultimate outlet in a real throat cutting—or in a nuclear holocaust. To rebel against the Name-of-the-Father, as Cohn rebels against God, is to be called by that name in one's turn. Sons kill their fathers, thus becoming fathers themselves, as in the dreary cycles of Greek mythology. Yet we must set this vision against a statement that Malamud once made to the effect that "the purpose of a writer is to keep civilization from destroying itself." In telling his story, then, he is a little like Calvin Cohn: "On good days Cohn told himself stories, saying the Lord would let him live if he spoke the right words" (1982, 10). No less than Cohn, Malamud the storyteller is caught in a vicious circle.

The resolution of this circle can only be the same one adopted to break the reciprocal and escalating patterns of violence in the primitive community: that of sacrifice. The tendency of sacrifice, we must remember, is always to move further away from the original spontaneous act by a process of substitution. An arbitrary victim substitutes for the community, and succeeding rituals substitute a designated and often willing victim for him. Then an animal is substituted for the human being, as in the story of Abraham and Isaac. A substitution beyond this one is possible and demonstrated in *God's Grace:* it is the sacrifice of the story, the sacrificial text.

3

The idea of the sacrificial text is the "thread of Ariadne," as Derrida has called it, which runs through Mark Taylor's *Altarity.* And since Taylor's book is a reading of Heidegger, Merleau-Ponty, Lacan, Bataille, Kristeva, Levinas, Blanchot, and Derrida (besides Hegel and Kierkegaard), we become aware of the degree to which this thread runs through much postmodern thinking. The book is moreover framed by the scene of sacrifice. The first section, on Hegel, has as its frontispiece—a visual preface, so to speak—Rembrandt's etching of *Abraham's Sacrifice*. The last section, on Kierkegaard, is prefaced with Chagall's painting of the same subject. The altar on which this sacrifice takes place is also the "alter"—the Other that is the concern of so much post-Hegelian thought.

The Other in this philosophical version is that which is excluded by the closed, self-sufficient Hegelian system, a system that turns all differences into identity, an identity that is ultimately that of the human self. Beyond that self, and thus beyond its comprehension, the Other is unthinkable. Attempts to explain it commonly resort to the language of paradox, a friction of irreconcilables which ends by exploding systematic thought. Language itself, which attempts to explain the Other, in the process discovers something of its own nature as a system. It cannot comprehend the Other, though otherness is in a certain sense that of which it is compounded: in Saussure's theory it is pure difference that makes up a linguistic system. The fullness of a text, philosophical or literary, is then always fissured by its other, by Otherness. This rift is akin to the *coupure* by which, according to Lacan, we enter the symbolic system. The *coupure* both opens our throat to language and fatally flaws that language. Yet a text that admits this and enacts it can make something more of that fatality: it can become a sacrificial text.

The violence of sacrifice, unlike that of murder or suicide, is linked to the sacred. In *Altarity* the sacred is in turn linked to the Other; Taylor is, after all, a theologian. His project is not, however, to reinstate an ontotheology, a godhead marked by presence, and moreover one derived from human notions of self-presence. Taylor argues for an "atheology" that might be summed up in these words of Kierkegaard: "If man is to receive any true knowledge about the Unknown (the God), he must be made to know that it is different from him, absolutely different from him" (1971, 55). This knowledge itself faults our notions of knowledge, tears open our comfortable ontology, which is in this manner sacrificed to the sacred.

Though such a sacrifice may take place first of all in religious ritual, more recently—according to both Julia Kristeva and Georges Bataille—it takes place in the writing of modern and postmodern artists. Kristeva asks "whether all writing is not a second order rite, at the level of language, which causes one to be reminded, through the linguistic signs themselves, of the demarcations that precondition them and exceed them. Writing, in effect, causes the subject who risks it to confront an archaic authority on the nether side of the proper Name" (1982, 178). After the death of God, then, literature remains to "take the place of the sacred." This is to establish not a religion of art, but an art that destroys itself to open a passageway to the inaccessible Other. *Poésie,* for instance, in Bataille's understanding of the term, "signifies, in the most precise way, creation by means of loss. Its meaning is therefore close to that of *sacrifice*" (1985, 120).

Opinions vary on what exactly is lost in a textual sacrifice. For Michel Foucault, "Writing is now linked to sacrifice" (1977, 117) through the death of the author, victimized by his own writing. For Walter Benjamin, in "The Storyteller," the sacrificial element is the death of the fictional protagonist: "What draws the reader to the novel is the hope of warming his shivering life with a death he reads about" (1968, 101). The protagonist is consumed like a burnt offering to heighten the life of the reader whose substitute he is. What consumes both Foucault's author, outside the text, and Benjamin's protagonist, inside it, is the text itself—a text that may be a self-consuming artifact. Its style, for one thing, may be yet another burnt offering, another form of sacrifice. So Derrida wishes for a language that "remains self-evidently secret . . . as if it were burning immediately" upon being read (1987,

11). And Kristeva wishes for a literary apocalypse that is not a "revelation," but rather is "black with burnt up meaning" (1980, 195). It is noteworthy that this apocalypse is arrived at by way of a style that Kristeva calls "carnivalesque." If a literary style may be said to be the mimesis of the spirit of carnival, in ways that we will not explore here, the carnival itself, according to Girard, is the socially approved mimesis of the sacrificial crisis, in which all the differences of a social structure are blurred. This crisis, like the institution of carnival, and like the texts of which Kristeva speaks, finds its resolution in some form of sacrifice: in Kristeva's theory the burnt offering is a purely literary one.

Author, protagonist, or writing itself may then enact the textual sacrifice. To various degrees, all three losses are involved in Malamud's last novel. Its protagonist is explicitly sacrificed; his body is burnt by a flame that is both a literal one and the figurative flame that, according to Benjamin, warms the reader. But it goes much beyond that. Words, in Malamud's novel, do not merely provide a mimetic representation of sacrifice—even a "symbolic" one. As we have seen, words close over the literally described sacrifice, seeming to nullify its meaning in a final ironical twist. Yet that twist, like so many in *God's Grace,* turns the story against itself. This story, which is a story about stories, in the end sacrifices the very *idea* of story—at least the comfortable idea, where there is a message to convey (like "Save Our Planet") and where we have a beginning, middle, and end. Malamud's narrative is deceptively simple, straightforwardly chronological, not in the least avant garde. But beneath it (if "beneath" is the right word) tensions and paradoxes, as we have seen, resist ordering by any comfortable sequence or logic. At this level the idea of ordering explodes and we have "time no more," as in the Book of Revelation. Malamud's book too is apocalyptic—and not just because it begins by speaking of a nuclear holocaust. It is a literary apocalypse in Julia Kristeva's terms, "black with burnt up meaning." The text itself is a burnt offering, a sacrificial text.

4

If we turn back now to the ending of *Gravity's Rainbow,* we find that it is likewise sacrificial. In the waning days of the war, Rocket 00001 is fired from Luneburg Heath. The commander has ordered modifications that will allow the body of the rocket to accommodate a passenger, a sacrificial victim introduced in the text by a brief meditation on Isaac. This victim is the boy Gottfried, the commander's paramour, dressed in the white of weddings or of death. His feet, in white satin slippers, are bound; he is gagged with a white kid glove. "A dim, whited room" (1973, 754), a shroud made of Imipolex, encases him. We follow countdown and then flashback as Gottfried's life passes before his eyes: versions of reversal, in a novel full of such versions. Yet when the rocket begins its fall on the far side of the arc that gravity gives, it flashes forward in time. It descends onto a city that is partly the Los Angeles of 1973 (the publication date of *Gravity's Rainbow*) and partly a futuristic City of unparalleled scope, vertically and horizontally: elevator trips have the duration of commuter train journeys, and stations on the underground are numbered by their years. Onto this City the rocket descends, and specifically into the interior of the Orpheus Theatre, which is experiencing technical difficulties. Whether because of broken film, or a burned-out bulb, "the screen is a dim page spread before us, white and silent." The metaphor in a sense reverses itself as we read it: the page becomes a dim screen, and we read the whiteness behind the print, the silence behind the words. That silence is a characteristic of the descending rocket: early in the novel we have been told that "it travels faster than the speed of sound. The first news you get of it is the blast. Then, if you're still around, you hear the sound of it coming in" (1973, 7). The novel's first sentence, then—"A screaming comes across the sky"—must be situated in the time *after.* And still proceeding backwards we come to the initial epigraph of the book, in which Wernher von Braun speaks of his faith in "the continuity of our spiritual existence after death." Though this sounds comfortingly religious, the novel that follows (if such a chronology applies) has a different tone. That tone evokes, if anything, the afterlife as envisioned by Alfred Jarry, who believed that the brain continued to dream after death, and that the dreams produced by its gradual decay were the source of an hallucinatory heaven or hell. The whiteness of the page underscores the fact that death is the source of the dream that is this novel.

This claim becomes more comprehensible in the context of Maurice Blanchot's writings, in particular *L'Espace Littéraire,* translated as *The Space of Literature.* As I will be dealing more with Blanchot in the next chapter, it may be enough here to say that the paradoxes of death—or rather of our relation/nonrelation with death—are seen by Blanchot as parallel to the paradoxes of writing. What, with careful qualification, he calls the "center" of his book (*pace* Derrida) is the essay on "The Gaze of Orpheus." In Blanchot's version of the Greek myth the writer, like Orpheus, must descend to the underworld, world of death and the ungraspable Other, if he is to write at all. His effort is to bring something of what he finds there to the light of day, or to the printed page. But paradoxically, if it can be said, it is already other than Other. Thus at the entrance to the daylight world Orpheus turns to look at what he has brought to light, and in the act of looking finds only disappearance. As he should. It is that very disappearance, the presence of an absence, that is his subject. Inherent in all writing, it can be evoked, if not captured, by certain strategies; and prominent among these is the act of *turning back.* That turning back is also a giving back of the work to its origins in the underworld. It is a gift, and it is a sacrifice.

> Orpheus's gaze is Orpheus's ultimate gift to the work. It is a gift whereby he refuses, whereby he sacrifices the work, bearing himself toward the origin according to desire's measureless movement—and whereby unknowingly he still moves toward the work, toward the origin of the work. (1982, 174)

The turn taken at the end of *Gravity's Rainbow* is sacrificial in this sense. The entire complex network of the novel's construction, like the destructive network it depicts, is now manifestly a "white network," as in Bodine's perception:

> In certain rushes now when he sees white network being cast in all directions on his field of vision, he understands it as an emblem of pain or death. (Pynchon 1973, 741)

These "rushes," in a punning way, are also film rushes; and the field of vision is that of the audience before a blank screen, staring at a manifested absence. And this too is the gaze of Orpheus. The patrons of the Orpheus Theatre are staring at the same Other as are the patrons of Pynchon. And this is so not only in the overarching pattern of the novel but at its most local manifestation—as we might guess from the last directions to "follow the bouncing ball." From word to word it bounces, inscribing each time the arc of a rise and fall, reminding us of the gravity of words, their pull downwards to the underworld from which the writer takes them, and to which the writer must return them in a sacrificial act.

5

A text, then, can be another substitution in a chain of substitutions for the primal sacrifice. But we have not yet come to the end of that chain. A text can only do violence to itself in the act of reading; and in that very act of reading a form of violence is accomplished in the reader, a violence that is also sacrificial. It is this kind of violence, perhaps, which Kafka was speaking of when he said that literature should come upon us like a catastrophe.

This experience of reading may also be read as a revision of Lacan's mirror stage. The mirror helped to provide the child's ego with its imaginary ideal, its totalized being. Now the child, grown old, must unlearn the lesson of its egoistic being and learn instead that which has determined it. And if it is language that has determined it, it is language that must, in a sense for the first time, be read. One must read reading. And in so doing one reads one's "self." One sees that self in the text, inscribed in textuality—sees its nature as in a mirror. Literature may thus enact a strange version of its Shakespearean function, to "hold the mirror up to nature." The sacrificial text holds the mirror up to human nature to reveal that it is not natural, or even what has been called "human." This mirror presents the subject with its deconstructed image, the reverse of the constructed subject that was falsely glimpsed in the mirror stage. And all this can be accomplished through language, in a text.

So, beyond one's assumption into the structures of language, another stage is possible: the recognition of that assumption. That recognition is the purpose of Lacanian psychoanalysis. Not that it "cures" us of our fated condition in any simple sense. With a sentence Lacan tells us all that can be done: "Psychoanalysis may accompany the patient to the ecstatic limit of the *'Thou art That,'* in which is revealed to him the cipher of his mortal destiny" (1977, 7). The "cipher" of his mortal destiny may be a riddle, a zero, a circle; but before it is any of these things it is a sign, one that reveals that it is our destiny to construct ourselves within a signifying system. That is the "that" to which the subject is pointed now, in contrast to the "that" of the mirror image. It is, in effect, the entire Lacanian theory. And the effect of that revelation is the deconstruction of the ego that the mirror stage first presented whole. This revelation is "ecstatic" in the etymological sense of that word, in which one "stands outside"; and what one stands outside of here is the self, or rather the very *idea* of "self." In the act of knowing how delusive—and how inevitable—the construction of that idea was in the beginning, the idea is sacrificed. Like any sacrifice, this is both an end and a regenerative beginning. Some of its regenerative nature can be glimpsed in these words of Emmanuel Levinas:

Modern antihumanism, which denies the primacy that the human person (free and for itself) would have for the signification of being, is true over and beyond the reasons it gives itself. It clears the place for subjectivity positing itself in abnegation, in sacrifice, in a substitution that precedes the will. The genius of its intuition is to have abandoned the idea of person, goal, and origin of itself, in which the ego is still a thing because it is still a being. . . . Humanism has to be denounced only because it is not sufficiently human. (1981, 127–28)

If this sacrifice of self (not to be confused with self-sacrifice) is the final "cure" of psychoanalysis, it may also be that of literature. After all, Lacan's psychoanalysis works through language—as did Freud's when it was not yet psychoanalysis but "the talking cure." The language of the text can also effect a kind of cure, if it is of the right kind: "The Lord would let him live if he spoke the right words." This sentence might be the very motto of Lacanian psychoanalysis. The Lord, the Father, must be manifested in his name—that name which slides into a continual following-after. Thus the subject must above all speak and, hearing that speech, may see its patterns and paradoxes, which are those of the subject's "own" unconscious. The very putting into quotation marks of what is the subject's own is part of the realization that "Thou art That." This realization sounds much like "This is that story," as it should. For both subject and story—for the subject *as* story—there is always a story that precedes, that is "that" rather than "this," that is "there" rather than "here," that is other than the text that we have called self.

All wars, Derrida tells us, have been waged in the name of something. But since nothing will survive a totalizing nuclear war, there can be no referent for any name. Such a war, Derrida claims, would become the first war to be waged in the name of the name itself (1984, 30–31). Now the only name broad enough to have this capacity is the Name of the Father, which we have taken to ourselves, and out of which we have made our selves. To be made more aware of the Name of the Father is also to be made more wary of it, and of us. As Pogo once said, "We have seen the enemy and he is us." Nuclear holocaust is capable of consuming humanity for the sake of a "principle" that is important only as a kingpin of the ego's structure. Withdrawing that kingpin before the fact, we dismantle the ego's construction by admitting that it is, precisely, constructed. Its patterns are those of a text that extends beyond the borders of self. Against this text I have set another: the sacrificial text. The sacrifice that it enacts may substitute for a coming holocaust that Derrida considers as yet another textual artifact. But "this is that story" only up to a point. And in the substitution that I have suggested of sacrifice for holocaust, identity must give way before a crucial difference.

3 IMAGINING HOPE

Disastrous Imagination

Continuing a series of returns, let us turn back to that hypothetical monument of empty space at the site of ground zero in Hiroshima, moving our investigation now not toward its unattainable center but toward that uneasy circumference that is us. If this monument, constructed through its absence, had been the one chosen, what would be the effect on its observers? Trying to imagine that empty space at the center of the city, we find only differences from the absolute absence it claims to represent: it fills with the shadow of passing clouds, the swoop of birds, blowing leaves, schoolchildren's voices. It fills above all with our own imaginings; the absence fills with our presence—which never reaches fulfillment. Because this monument gives us no form for our responses, we are made more aware of how responses are drawn out of us without resolution or revelation, no apocalypse.

This is perhaps the most disturbing thing about an initial encounter with the nuclear problem, no matter from what point of entry. Responses proliferate bewilderingly, and *they are not our responses:* they pull us toward a realm that is other than that of our "proper" selves, that is the absence of our selves and the presence of an Other. Not surprisingly, the usual response is to foreclose the process: by dogmatism, by denial.

The difficult process of encountering an extreme Otherness informs all of the work of Maurice Blanchot. And of his many books, the one that most concerns this book is *The Writing of the Disaster.* Admittedly, the disaster referred to is not explicitly that of nuclear holocaust: it is the Jewish Holocaust that provides Blanchot's examples, on the few occasions when he uses an example. For such historical disasters are manifestations in time of that which is outside time—in fact the idea of "the outside" itself is an important aspect of what Blanchot is talking about. "The Disaster" is a metaphor for the complete undoing of all human conceptions. It is that which is outside of all notions of self or of cosmic order projected by self. "There is a question, and nothing that can be said, but just this nothing, to say" (1986, 9). To name it as nothingness is then one way of talking about the disaster—a misleading way, however, if that idea is given an existential glamour as an ultimate antagonist; for antagonism presupposes the existence of something that is being acted against, a positive to set against the negative. Rather the disaster is *le neutre*—the ultimate indifference behind *différance.*

Because it is wholly outside of the human, and of human patterns of meaning, the disaster cannot be defined or represented. It is "that which, in thought, cannot make itself present, or enter into presence, and is still less able to be represented or to constitute itself as a basis for representation" (1986, 33). However, the disaster can up to a point be evoked by certain strategies favored by Blanchot: fragmentation, repetition, the making and unmaking of metaphor. In these ways Blanchot avoids the danger "that the disaster acquire meaning instead of body" (1986, 41). As with many contemporary theoreticians, his writing devours itself. Indeed, he believes that writing is something one cannot do, if that means finding the words for the disaster, for that which cannot be said. Yet, as Merleau-Ponty once observed, we are constantly living the solution to problems that reason cannot solve. So writing is done, and by Blanchot more than most. This is so, doubtless, because he is *fascinated*—in a sense that Blanchot tries to convey in a number of ways in his essay "The Essential Solitude." For instance:

> To write is to let fascination rule language. It is to stay in touch, through language, in language, with the absolute milieu where the thing becomes image again, where the image, instead of alluding to some particular feature, becomes an allusion to the featureless, and instead of a form drawn upon absence, becomes the formless presence of this absence, the opaque, empty opening onto that which is when there is no more world, when there is no world yet. (1982, 33)

In a sense this writing is the reverse of the apocalyptic, which always supposes a world's presence before that presence can be ended. Here what fascinates us is simply that which is not-world: "What fascinates robs us of our power to give sense" (1982, 32). By "sense" Blanchot here means not only meaning but the sensory, that which makes the world that disaster unmakes. The writing he speaks of and is fascinated by is never given body, undercut as it is by Blanchot's strategies and its own innate disaster. That disaster, on the other hand, acquires its own kind of body, "formless presence of this absence." Such a paradoxical writing is explained at one point in language that is again paradoxical: "There passes through this sentence what it can contain only by bursting" (1986, 116).

The enabling metaphor of the sentence just quoted is that of an explosion. It is not a wholly new comparison. T. S. Eliot implied something similar when he compared the writer's activity to the injection of chemicals into a closed chamber. And Blanchot frequently quotes Stéphane Mallarmé's claim that "there is no explosion except a book." But in the 1990s Blanchot's metaphor may convey something quite different from what it did in the 1890s—just as the *Quixote* of Pierre Menard, in Jorge Luis Borges's well-known story, while preserving Cervantes's exact words, is a very different piece of literature. The explosion evoked may now be the ultimate one of a nuclear holocaust—and all the more so because of its bond with ultimate absence, the disaster of an annihilation that manifests only an utter indifference to all human structures of meaning.

When Blanchot quotes Mallarmé in *The Writing of the Disaster* he adds an explanation:

> This means that the book is not the laborious assembling of a totality finally obtained, but has for its being the noisy, silent bursting which without the book would not take place (would not affirm itself). (1986, 124)

Blanchot omits, however, some lines that appeared in his first version of this passage: a brief untranslated essay entitled "Il n'est d'explosion . . .": "Here, where the little atomic flashes are postponed in their modest capacity, episodic manifestations of the only explosion which is the book, the book denounces its status of totality" (1978, 11)—without, we might add, renouncing its total monopoly on explosion. Now, in *The Writing of the Disaster,* Blanchot considers this possible link to the atomic only once, only parenthetically, and only to dismiss it: "I will add that none of the current images of the death drive (the atomic threat etc.) has anything to do with the unrepresentable aspect of the death drive" (1986, 118–19). It is true that such public images are inadequate as *representations;* and that the ultimate indifference Blanchot refers to as the disaster is not a mere by-product of the nuclear age. Nevertheless, the atomic threat is perhaps the most powerful contemporary manifestation of that terrible indifference. It touches with a shiver of awareness people who have never heard of Blanchot, who wouldn't give a damn for literary theory or even for literature. It touches Blanchot as well, perhaps more than he thinks—as is the case with all of us. "They do not think of death, having no other relation but with death," writes Blanchot (1986, 40). He is emphasizing how a force that is pervasive becomes invisible to those for whom it is their element; and he is not exempt from the point that he is making.

Theoreticians build their own monuments to Hiroshima,

whether consciously or not. So the metaphors used in *The Writing of the Disaster* reflect the destructive element in which its writer, like all of us, is immersed. The invisible and escalating pressure of nuclearism in the 1970s may have played its part in moving Blanchot away from the metaphors he first used to express his preoccupations with writing. In "The Gaze of Orpheus" the classical myth of Orpheus and Euridyce becomes emblematic of the poet's relation to the abyss from which he draws his words and to which he consigns them again. But that abyss is still something of a pâpier-maché Hades. In *The Writing of the Disaster* the metaphor has changed, even though its referent may seem to be the same. The abyss is now without location, defined only by its absence. Two so-called "primal scenes" evoke it in terms reminiscent of Magritte. The experience

> breaks, by the smashing of a pane (behind which one rests assured of perfect, of protected visibility), the finite-infinite space of the cosmos—ordinary order—the better to substitute the knowing vertigo of the deserted outside. (1986, 115)

The smashed pane (of the sky, in the other version of this scene) recalls Magritte's painting *On the Threshold of Liberty* (fig. 4). We see a room made up of large panes, and those panes are such things as sky, flesh, and forest. In the room is a large cannon reared up on its carriage and pointing at the pane of sky. Past this threshold moment can only be an explosion; and past that, Blanchot's "outside."

But the metaphorical resonances of the book do not end with surrealism in a work that is poststructuralist, postmodern, and preapocalyptic. Blanchot's "explosion" and "disaster" are of our time and implicated (as is that time) with the nuclear subject. So contemporary works attempting to deal with that subject often, consciously or not, put Blanchot's theories into practice. Of course, Blanchot himself does this, in a series of disturbing novels. As for writing in English, the most direct case of his influence is Paul Auster, who besides being a novelist is a scholar

4 René Magritte, *Au seuil de la liberté* (*On the Threshold of Liberty*), 1929. Museum Boymans-van Beuningen, Rotterdam. Permission granted to reproduce.

and sometime translator of Blanchot: Auster's *In the Country of Last Things,* for instance, is pervaded with the echo of disaster, possibly nuclear. Most uncanny, however, is the way that many works with no direct lineage to Blanchot's ideas begin to exemplify them, under the pressure of the nuclear Other.

1

In his essay on "The Song of the Sirens" Blanchot speculates on the nature of the sirens' song and its fatal attraction, using terms that echo his ideas on the fascination of writing:

> The enchantment held out an enigmatic promise and through this promise exposed men to the danger of being unfaithful to

themselves, unfaithful to their human song and even to the essence of song, by awakening in them hope and a desire for a
marvellous beyond, and that beyond was only a desert, as
though the region where music originated was the only place
completely without music, a sterile dry place where silence, like
noise, burned all access to the song in anyone who had once
had command of it. (1981, 106)

The imagery here recalls (or to be precise anticipates) an actual
piece of music, Steve Reich's *The Desert Music* (1984). The desert
referred to in its title is, as in Blanchot, not a place but a state—
and not so much a state of mind as a place for encountering that
which is outside of mind. Traditionally, deserts have threatened
normal thinking, Reich explains. He cites the desert of Sinai
where the Jews received divine revelations; Jesus' sojourn in the
desert to be tempted by the devil; and finally White Sands and
Almagordo in New Mexico, where nuclear testing takes place.
The text, made up of passages from William Carlos Williams,
centers around this one written in response to nuclear testing:
"Man has survived hitherto because he was too ignorant to know
how to realize his wishes. Now that he can realize them, he must
either change them or perish." Yet rather than providing words
to be set to music, this text, along with others by Williams, func-
tioned as a "goad" for the composer; the texts do not dominate the
music itself. "That constant flickering of attention between what
words mean and how they sound when set to music is one main
focus of *The Desert Music*," Reich has said in his notes to the
recording. A steady pulsation carries us into and out of the piece,
recurring at intervals along with other shifting repetitions that
create in the listeners a "desert place"; here they encounter nuclear themes, through musical themes, with a perception akin to
fascination.

Reich's piece is a version in sound of what Blanchot has described in terms of sight: "What happens is not an active contact,
not the initiative and action which there still is in real touching.
Rather, the gaze gets taken in, absorbed by an immobile move-

ment and a depthless deep" (1982, 32). These last phrases accurately render the effect of Reich's minimalist techniques, in particular the repetition that is a technique of Blanchot as well. In this way "access to the song" is denied, perhaps, but not access to a burning silence behind it. At the same time the tension mentioned by Reich between words and music is paralleled by another tension. The passage from Williams challenges its hearers to change and (perhaps like the phenomenon of change itself) hovers between "inner" and "outer" worlds: one's inner wishes may now be realized, made real in the world. The music, as I read it, reverses this movement and calls into question this terminology. For now the "outside" calls into question the world of sense and action, evoking a wasteland from which we cannot avert our fascinated gaze. Between words and music, in that very "flickering of attention" of which Reich speaks, the hearer of *The Desert Music* may negotiate, not easily, a psychological coming to terms that is also a nuclear agreement.

Another minimalist composer, Philip Glass, uses similar techniques and tensions in *Einstein on the Beach,* the opera he wrote with Robert Wilson. Its libretto is for the most part abstract: solfège is used when the composer wishes to bring out the pattern of intervals between notes; counting is used when he wishes to emphasize the rhythmic pattern. What language there is in the opera is at two extremes, each calling into question the notion of communicable meaning. At one extreme there is banality, language that is dying or dead ("Paris is one of the world's greatest tourist attractions. And not without reason, for Paris has much to offer"). At the other extreme are the writings of a sixteen-year-old autistic boy ("Will it get some wind for the sailboat. And it could be were it is"). Blanchot would particularly approve of the latter language: "He who no longer knows how to write, who renounces the gift which he has received, whose language is unrecognizable, is closer to the untried experience, closer to the absence of the 'proper' which, even without being, gives place to the advent" (1986, 99). What kind of advent Blanchot is referring to here becomes clearer through a consideration of the techniques in the opera by which that advent is produced.

Philip Glass's minimalism means that his compositions accumulate out of small units repeated at great length with subtle, evolving changes. Similarly Blanchot's composition exemplifies an aesthetic of fragmentation and repetition. The fragment, he says, "maintains itself as the energy of disappearing: a repetitive energy . . . the presence of the work of art's absence (to say it all again and to silence by saying it again)" (1986, 60–61). He refers to "the repeated, motionless step of the speechless unknown, there at our door, on the threshold" (1986, 39). If the libretto is one way of indicating the speechless unknown through inadequacy of speech, another way is through the series of images on which Robert Wilson bases the opera. Elemental, fraught, these images progress not in any sequence of plot or conscious aesthetic pattern but with the logic of dreams. Train, trial, prison, building, bed, spaceship—and linking all of these the figure of Einstein as the solo violinist. One could find explanations for these images—the train as a popular example of relativity, the spaceship as the unexplored possibilities of Einstein's new universe, and so on—but such pat explanations are rapidly undermined by the repetitions of Glass's music, which hypnotically move us beyond the conscious and rational. It is at the level of the unconscious, then, that we are enabled to come to terms with the dilemma evoked by the allusion in the opera's title to Nevil Shute's novel of nuclear destruction. Because the bomb has penetrated our unconscious in so many ways, it is perhaps at that level that we must come to terms with it first.

Blanchot would, of course, distrust this psychoanalytic terminology, for he feels that the idea of the unconscious has been used to cover the abyss of the disaster. Let us say, then, that the whole of *Einstein on the Beach* takes place at the "outer edges" and produces a corresponding kind of knowledge.

Knowledge becomes finer and lighter only at the outer edges, when truth no longer constitutes the principle to which it must finally submit . . . [There] knowledge, without passing into unknowledge, no longer depends upon itself, and neither results nor produces a result, but changes imperceptibly, effacing itself. (Blanchot 1986, 42–43)

Through the slow evolution of the opera, through its repetitions which continually annihilate what has preceded, the disaster is made manifest, and most of all in its nuclear form. In a work remarkable as much for its absences as for its presences, and which may even be thought of as a repeated series of absences, there is room for each member of the audience to arrive at an individual negotiation with that disastrous absence, if not at a final resolution. Certainly the opera's cumulative effect over five hours produces something like Mallarmé's explosion: in the premiere performance, after the first couple of hours, a simple key change sent waves of screaming through the audience. But the real explosion is within, in that knowledge which abolishes our ideas of knowledge, which is other than mastery or coherence, knowledge of the disaster buried not within concrete silos in the ground but within the abyss of ourselves.

2

Einstein on the Beach reminds us of something we continually forget; yet forgetting is itself a way to that knowledge and may even *be* that knowledge. "The disaster is related to forgetfulness," Blanchot declares, "forgetfulness without memory, the motionless retreat of what has not been treated—the immemorial, perhaps" (1986, 3). Forgetting is the central concern of Denis Johnson's *Fiskadoro,* both in its usual sense and in Blanchot's special sense:

And what is forgetfulness? It is not related to ignorance of the eventual present (the future) any more than it is loss of the memorable from the memory. Forgetfulness designates that

which is beyond possibility, the unforgettable Other; it indicates
that which, past or future, it does not circumscribe: patience in
its passive mode. (Blanchot 1986, 117)

At its simplest level, forgetting, loss of memory, is one of a
whole series of losses in Johnson's novel. The largest of these
losses is indicated by its postapocalyptic setting: *Fiskadoro* takes
place after the End of the World, as it is referred to by the inhabitants of the only part of the United States to be spared, the Flor-
ida Keys. Two nuclear warheads have landed on Key West, but
because neither exploded the place is now called Twicetown, and
the bombs lie in the fields in a ritual isolation. To the north everything is dead, is the source of death in smuggled, radioactive
goods. To the south are the Cubans, who will take over as soon as
the Quarantine expires. Within this world of loss, thirteen-year-
old Fiskadoro loses his father, a fisherman, to the sea; he loses his
mother to cancer; he returns from his abduction by the neighbor-
ing "swamp people" having lost his memory as the aftermath of
a drug-laden ritual practiced upon him. At the end of the book his
paltry society is lost, as is a war from before the End of the World,
when the Cubans finally arrive. Yet, appropriating Blanchot's
words here, "to speak of loss, of pure loss, and in pure loss,
seems, even though speech is never secure, still too facile" (1986,
50). Rather than assimilating forgetfulness into this pattern of
loss, it is more fruitful to pursue its own ramifications.

The concept of forgetfulness links Fiskadoro to two other
characters: Mr. Cheung, the manager of a ragtag band known as
the Miami Symphony Orchestra; and Mr. Cheung's grandmother,
well over a hundred now, last survivor of the End of the World.
Mr. Cheung (he is always referred to in this respectful manner)
"believed in the importance of remembering" (1985, 10). Early in
the novel he demonstrates his mnemonic technique for remembering the names of the fifty states, long since gone; and he can
recite the whole Declaration of Independence, including the
punctuation and signatures. His business is to preserve the past:

"I stand against the forces of destruction, against the forces that took the machines away" (1985, 123). More than anything else, this means the atomic bomb, linked with forgetting: "As the bombs fell, already we were forgotten. The bomb said, I will not remember" (1985, 153). Ironically, knowledge of what happened at the End of the World is confusedly gleaned from an old copy of Frank W. Chinnock's *Nagasaki: The Forgotten Bomb.* Mr. Cheung, who wants above all to remember, has moments of self-doubt: "What are my forces? With what am I aligned? I am not aligned with anything real, only the past. I am against everything" (1985, 117).

Mr. Cheung's grandmother has lived that past, but her memories are erratic and in any case incommunicable: "The nearest she came to speech was to form various silences with her lips" (1985, 12). To her grandson it is "as if she forgot everything as soon as it happened" (1985, 32). What she does remember only ends up reasserting the primacy of forgetting in Blanchot's widest sense. On one of her clearer days she is "flinging herself onto these memories as onto a solid place" (1985, 206). Yet her memories are of the crash of a helicopter into the China sea after escaping from the fall of Saigon, and of two days of trying to keep afloat in that sea, where there is nothing to cling to: "the China sea looked like nothing . . . something enormous, engulfing, mind-erasing, seen only in series, swell after swell, too absolutely filled with itself to admit any mercy, to know its name or take any thought" (1985, 209). Sleepless, exhausted, always only inches from drowning, "She could not forget herself without dying. Nevertheless she forgot herself" (1985, 215). This sequence is the most extended exploration of a metaphor that surfaces repeatedly in the book. Fiskadoro's father is drowned; his society will follow ("One day someday Babylon go sink down deadndrowned-oh"); and when a boy of the swamp people drowns near Twicetown, Fiskadoro is abducted to replace him and subsequently forgets all of his past.

Fiskadoro is made one of the swamp people through the ritual of subincision, in which the underside of the penis is slit open. He is prepared for this operation by a massive outpouring of words, all of which he must remember and recite back to the tribal elders. Through the agency of the drugs he has been administered, he is able to accomplish this prodigious feat of memory, before losing all memory completely. In a parallel fashion, the excess of words—he feels he is drowning in them—culminates in silence. The words themselves indicate the movement to forgetfulness:

> "When the earth is crushed to fine dust, and your Lord comes down with the angels, in their ranks, and Hell is brought near—on that day man will remember his deeds. But what will memory avail him? . . . You touch the people and they dissolve. There is nothing left but you. And you will not remember." (1985, 183)

There are apostrophes to the "Formless, Non-existent, Imperishable, and Transcendent Fullness of the Emptiness; the Voidness; the Eternal God" and to his prophet Mohammed, and to the power that he brings, which is "the power to go on living after Hell is brought near, the power to make babies and keep generations living on the Earth" (1985, 183, 180).

From this, the significance of the subincision becomes clear. It is a mimicry of the female sexual organs, an appropriation by the male of the female power of generation, as Bruno Bettelheim explicates the ritual in his *Symbolic Wounds*. But in the context of Denis Johnson's novel, subincision has additional significance that links it to the notion of forgetfulness. That which a woman has between her legs is "nothing," as in Shakespeare. But far from being a derogatory nothing, the female sexual organ has a metaphorical relationship to "the Emptiness, the Voidness" which is "Eternal God." Out of such a nothing, and only from that nothing, can come the power to generate the world—or to regenerate it after "Hell is brought near." To make this possible, phallic power must be undercut, both literally and figuratively. So memory, consciousness, and control must go. Fiskadoro must forget, and he must incorporate within himself the principle of forgetting, just as his body incorporates the hole that is its symbol.

When he is brought back to Twicetown there are hints of Fiskadoro's new creative power. Before his abduction, he has been taking lessons on the clarinet from Mr. Cheung, who perseveres even though he knows the boy has no talent. Now he plays better than his teacher: "He forgot himself and turned into music" (1985, 207). He can also read now in a way he was never capable of before: "Sometimes . . . instead of marks on a page Fiskadoro saw images in his mind" (1985, 195). The reader of this novel is momentarily made to remember how much forgetting is necessary in order to read at all. Most broadly, Fiskadoro is a new generation, beyond Mr. Cheung and beyond his grandmother. According to the Cuban narrator for whom the book's events belong to the historical past, Fiskadoro is "the only one who was ready when we came" (1985, 12). He is able to regenerate the world after its nuclear Hell—not by reconstructing the world out of what has been preserved, as Mr. Cheung wishes to do, but by finding within the principle of disaster itself the source of creation.

3

"You are beginning to follow the relation between a certain brandished erection and a certain head of speech that is cut off, the brand or pole rising up in the manifestation of the cut, incision, split, break, scission" (Derrida 1981, 302). Derrida's figure of speech here is literalized not only in *Fiskadoro* but in another novel on the psychology of our relation to the bomb, Tim O'Brien's *The Nuclear Age*. As a result of a childhood accident, a bicycle spill, the narrator ends up with a "mangled pecker." A doctor botches the repair job: "He put in these huge stitches, like railway ties, and I've still got the scar on my pecker to prove it. Great big tread marks, as if I'd been sewn up by a blind man"

(1985, 19). The sign of the cut is manifested upon or within the sign of the signifier, the phallus as signifier; the cut is akin to Lacan's *coupure.*

The disparity of tone between the narrator's statement and my academic comment on it is worth a second look. William Cowling, the narrator of *The Nuclear Age,* writes in a style that I have elsewhere called "the language of men": conversational, even colloquial; slangy; occasionally foul-mouthed; and above all anti-literary. Cowling is like those male writers who belong to what Shulamith Firestone has called a twentieth-century School of Virility—Mailer is the most prominent example—in feeling that literature is an effeminate activity. A style must then be evolved that will fend off the threat of emasculation, that will turn pen into penis. In Cowling's case, his "normal," "American," "manly" style is defensive on many fronts. It—he—is set against his wife's work as a poet, whose poems (pinned to his pajamas, stapled to the cereal box) try to turn him away from his unhealthy obsession with nuclear armageddon. "No metaphor, the bombs are real," he insists (1985, 4). What he fails to see is that a reality may simultaneously function as a metaphor; and that metaphor is related to psychological symptom.

Throughout the book Cowling is engaged in an action that is both metaphor and symptom. It is 1995 and he is digging a hole in his back yard to use as a fallout shelter. The novel alternates between the present, the effect his present activity is having on his family, and Cowling's memories of his past, the lifelong search for security which has brought him to this moment. His life story thus emerges out of an absence, and, moreover, a nuclear one. The hole takes on a character of its own, ironic and hip, conscious of its own paradoxical nature:

> *Hey, man,* the hole whispers. *Here's a riddle: What is here but not here, there but not there?* Then a pause. "You," I say, and the hole chuckles: *Oh, yeah! I am the absence of presence. I am the presence of absence. I am peace everlasting.* (1985, 198)

The fact that the hole *talks* to the narrator naturally raises the question that opens the book: "Am I crazy?" To answer this question one must put oneself in the position of the psychoanalyst, suspending judgment over the whole course of the novel's monologue, allowing the live American idiom to manifest the gaps and fissures within it, and coming to realize that these are not unconnected to the hole that is the literalized symptom of Cowling's paranoia. A good Lacanian might see parallels to the paradigmatic case of paranoia, that of Daniel Schreber as it is analyzed in "A Question Preliminary to Any Possible Treatment of Psychosis." Complex as that analysis is, it centers around the concept of a hole left by the incomplete movement of a metaphor. Metaphor is defined by Lacan simply as "signifying substitution" (1977, 200); and the specific metaphor at stake here is that of the "Name-of-the-Father," which acquires its significance from being substituted in the place opened by the mother's absence. If that substitution does not take place (is foreclosed), the Lacanian schema of the psyche is distorted. Certain lines of relation are now "conceived as circumventing the hole dug in the field of the signifier by the foreclosure of the Name-of-the-Father" (Lacan 1977, 205). This hole is also a hole "at the place of the phallic signification" (1977, 201), of the phallus as signifier. Without fully explicating Lacan's arguments on the Schreber case, or fully analyzing the Cowling case along similar lines, I wish only to emphasize the uncanny literalization in Cowling's life of certain metaphors in the psyche, which indeed composes itself by a metaphoric process.

But the very title of O'Brien's novel reminds us that we are not dealing with one case history; rather, history is the case. The hole then evokes some of the fundamental paradoxes of the nuclear age. It is dug for the sake of security. But in the course of the novel the hole changes from a defense against the nuclear threat to a personification of it. Cowling has always sought security, from the time as a boy when he turned the family Ping-Pong table into a fallout shelter to this moment in 1995 when he launches into the same project on a larger scale. But the hole eventually mocks all notions of shelter, tempting him instead with destruction, an absence that is "peace everlasting." Huge as the fallout shelter becomes, there is never a roof on it. Into the hole Cowling deposits his drugged wife and daughter, and he wires up a charge of dynamite: the explosion which is the ultimate avatar of the hole will allow him to "keep" them. The wheel has turned its full vicious circle. The hole is now that which, in William's childhood, initiated the quest for security with a frightening vision of nuclear holocaust:

> the melted elements of nature coursing into a single molten stream that roared outward into the very center of the universe— everything—man and animal—*everything*—the great genetic pool, everything, all swallowed up by a huge black hole. (1985, 30–31)

The ontological status of this hole, and of the nuclear end it images, is problematical. The bombs are real, Derrida admits in "No Apocalypse, Not Now," while arguing that nuclear holocaust is not. "Nuclear war has no precedent," he states. "It has never occurred, itself; it is a non-event. The explosion of American bombs in 1945 ended a 'classical' conventional war; it did not set off a nuclear war" (1984, 23). If Hiroshima and Nagasaki are forgotten in this manner, nuclear reality becomes a construct in language, fabulously textual. Even if it were to come to pass, a nuclear war would bring with it "no apocalypse"; for in its total and irreversible destruction, it would obliterate memory and even comprehension. So Cowling muses, "When it happens . . . it will not happen, because it cannot happen. It will not be *real*" (O'Brien 1985, 60). The only reality we can now deal with is that which is constructed by the fable of nuclear war. Even real bombs are constructed by this imaginary, according to Derrida, as is the overall shape of the epoch: "'Reality,' let's say the encompassing institution of the nuclear age, is constructed by the fable, on the basis of an event that has never happened (except in fantasy, and that is not nothing at all)." Derrida's footnote alludes to the letter to Fliess: "Freud said as early as 1897 that there was no difference in the unconscious between reality and a fiction loaded with affect" (1984, 27). The real then not only may be found within the dream, as Lacan suggests, but may be shaped by that dream—in whatever form it takes, including the literary.

Within "the encompassing institution of the nuclear age" is the fantasy that constructs it; within *The Nuclear Age,* a "fiction loaded with affect," lies a fantasy that likewise constructs the novel's realities. The fantasy, vision, or hallucination of nuclear destruction is by any normal definition unreal, yet it is "not nothing at all." In searching for words to describe its status, it is tempting to use those the hole has used, describing itself as "the presence of absence." Blanchot has used the same words, while immediately qualifying them, to describe a certain effect of the literary work which "points us constantly back to the presence of absence—but to this presence as absence, to absence as its own affirmation (an affirmation in which nothing is affirmed, in which nothing never ceases to affirm itself with the exhausting insistence of the indefinite" (1982, 30). In Cowling's vision there is nothing of the indefinite and even less of the unceasing: it is, precisely, an apocalypse, revelation of a nuclear end. And it is a revelation made to one who *sees.* The black hole's absence is made present to a presence, to one whose proper self remains untouched by disaster, who stands outside of Blanchot's "outside." Moreover, the ultimate forgetting manifested by the black hole is situated within a context of remembering, as Cowling's memories of that hallucinated black hole impel his digging of a real hole in the present. A more genuine act of remembering forgetfulness is that entailed in psychoanalysis.

The very existence of the unconscious is inferred from moments of forgetfulness, as exemplified in Freud's *Psychopathology of Everyday Life.* Psychoanalysis encourages us not so much to remember what has been forgotten as to remember forgetting. Which side of this paradoxical task you underscore perhaps determines whether you will choose Lacanian psychoanalysis or American ego psychology. If the latter, you are emphasizing memory in its aspect of prudence and control. According to Blanchot, memory—in contrast to the "immemorial" disaster—"frees me by giving me the means of calling freely upon the past, of ordering it according to my present intention" (1982, 30). Thus it is "my" intention that is empowered here; memory is in the service of the ego. It is that ego which must be relinquished in the encounter with a very different kind of power, an encounter that takes place notably in the scene of writing:

> The work requires of the writer that he lose everything he
> might construe as his own "nature," that he lose all character
> and that, ceasing to be linked to others and to himself by the
> decision which makes him an "I," he become the empty place
> where the impersonal affirmation emerges. (Blanchot 1982, 55)

What is enacted is a reversal of Freud's *Wo Es war, soll Ich werden* (Where Id was, Ego shall be), whose cooptation by ego psychology was attacked by Lacan in "The Freudian Thing." The unconscious affirms itself as impersonal; it is not there to be enlisted in any affirmative action of the ego.

Yet to say this does not mean that the unconscious is merely a determined and determining past, whose manifestation is not a force for change. There is in it an impulse to the future even where there is also in it that which blocks the impulse. The best example of this idea is doubtless the repetition compulsion that so puzzled Freud in *Beyond the Pleasure Principle*. What would account for the persistent return in shell-shocked soldiers of the memories they should be most concerned to get behind them? What, if not the aspect of the unconscious that impels it toward that which is before? The very form of repetition indicates that such is the case, for it is not a static remembering. As Kierkegaard observes: "Repetition and recollection are the same movement, only in opposite directions; for what is recollected has been, is repeated backwards, whereas repetition properly so called is recollected forwards" (1964, 53). To "recollect forwards" is what is attempted in the psychoanalytic process; and it is perhaps only through repetition that this form of recollection is possible. As in any narrative, the monologue of the subject derives its signification from the play of sameness and difference, the recognition of repetitive patterns that manifest themselves only as patterns in language. The "work" of psychoanalysis thus makes the same demands as does the writer's work, described by Blanchot above. In the space where ego was, an "impersonal affirmation" emerges which, being impersonal, is also a forgetting in Blanchot's sense. Forgetfulness has manifested itself through an act of remembering—no single act, but the cumulative effect of a series of steps, the same step that can never be the same, whose irrecoverability thus questions and consumes the very idea of memory, forgetting it while remembering forgetfulness.

Such a movement is enacted in O'Brien's novel, which I have already suggested may be seen as a psychoanalytic process. We have read the passage where Cowling remembers the ultimate forgetting of a nuclear end, which from the beginning rules his life. Yet by the end of the book Cowling has found another beginning; and in the place where a nuclear explosion generated the obsessive patterns of his psyche there is now an explosion in Blanchot's sense, or Mallarmé's. That explosion is generated by the repetitive patterns of Cowling's narrative, where time is marked by the rise and fall, *fort:da,* of shoveling: *Dig,* says the hole, and it might just as well be a psychoanalytic imperative. In any case it is an imperative that is generated by a concern for the future: that there *be* a future in the nuclear age, in the psyche of those who live in that age.

This future must be constructed in fantasy. "The future," Cowling tells us, "is always invented. You make it up out of air. And if you can't imagine it . . . it can't happen" (O'Brien 1985, 229). At one point, then, madness is described as a failure of the imagination, and the consequent loss of the real.

If you're crazy, I now understood, you don't feel grief or sad-
ness, you just can't find the future. . . . If you're crazy, it's a
lapse of the imagination. . . . You can't generate happy endings.
. . . If you're crazy, it's the end of the world. (1985, 232–33)

For such reasons as these, Cowling concludes that "the hole is
what we have when imagination fails" (1985, 306).

Yet are we to take this as the final word? Its binary oppositions
are a little too pat: a venerable tradition links, sometimes equates,
"craziness" and "imagination." In O'Brien's book both are manifested positively, negatively, in the end paradoxically. If their
fluctuations in meaning were sine curves, there would be intervals in which the two would reinforce each other, chime together;
at other intervals the two would diverge, pull away from each
other. One early symptom of madness is that Cowling sees missiles rising from their silos into the sky, sees nuclear submarines
surfacing, sees dying cities melt and flashes expand into space.
These are visions; and William Blake, who knew what he was
talking about, tells all of us who are sane, "You can see as I see.
Raise imagination to the point of vision and the thing is done."
But in the nuclear age sanity and madness form one vicious
circle: "If you're sane, you see madness. If you see madness, you
freak. If you freak, you're mad" (O'Brien 1985, 184).

Such vicious circularity is both pattern and image in Blanchot.
The work is a "pure circle" (1982, 52) that has at its center a zero;
this is both the work's origin and its disastrous end. And awareness of the disaster is the work's end in two senses, simultaneously destroying and fulfilling it. It is this kind of awareness that
Cowling attains at the end of *The Nuclear Age.* In accordance
with the promptings of the hole, Cowling rigs up dynamite, his
finger hovers over an actual button, everything he loves is within
that hole, within that moment on the threshold of annihilation.
The explosion that takes place, however, takes place within himself. For the hole's voice, we realize, is his voice, its emptiness is
his emptiness, and "the hole, it seems, is in my heart" (O'Brien

1985, 306). So what explodes is an act of the imagination, the imagination that makes a future possible. The psychological forces embodied in William Cowling have reached a "critical mass" that might well have impelled his finger to the button; instead, a regenerative act takes place, creating out of nothing even while knowing that nothing is what there is. In his madness Cowling has been "beside himself"—that is to say, outside of self, and inside the outside, Blanchot's outside. If he now "comes to himself," it is not the same self, nor is it a self separate from the disaster, in retreat from it, seeking security from it. Cowling remains aware that "Reality . . . tends to explode" (1985, 200). The vicious circle of sanity-insanity is resolved (if that is the right term) in an equally circular formulation: "To live is to lose everything, which is crazy, but I choose it anyway, which is sane" (1985, 310).

The form of this statement suggests a link with Blanchot's idea of "passivity," which can be evoked "only in language that reverses itself" (1986, 14). For merely to name passivity is not sufficient, suggesting that what is meant is the contrary of activity. But what Blanchot is aiming at is not a contrary of any kind; it is allied with the ultimate indifference. "We are passive with respect to the disaster," Blanchot says, "but the disaster is perhaps passivity" (1986, 3). That disaster is represented in the novel by the hole, and by a variety of ways in which Cowling is passive with respect to it. From obeying the dictates of the hole, Cowling moves to a realization that the hole is in himself. In accepting this metaphor he frees himself from the literalized version he has dug as a shelter from the nuclear age, which in the end only exemplifies that age. Instead of blowing up his wife and daughter according to the hole's directions, he takes them out of the hole and then destroys it in its own terms, through an explosion. He draws back from the threshold of a real disaster, choosing rather a disastrous endurance. He will suffer the passion that is one aspect of Blanchot's "passivity"; this may be understood as a component of any real responsibility, as Levinas has suggested:

Responsibility goes beyond being. In sincerity, in frankness, in
the veracity of this saying, in the uncoveredness of suffering,
being is altered. But this saying remains, in its activity, a passivity, more passive than all passivity, for it is a sacrifice without
reserve, without holding back, and in this it is non-voluntary.
(1981, 15)

Cowling incorporates within himself what he knows of the "outside" in a remembering of forgetfulness, in a sane acceptance of
madness. In his own way he has come to the same conclusion as
does Lacan in his study of psychosis: "Not only can man's being
not be understood without madness, it would not be man's being
if it did not bear madness within itself as the limit of his freedom"
(Lacan 1977, 215).

O'Brien's novel thus concludes with an affirmation whose content is paradoxical, produced by a kind of spontaneous combus-
tion of the emotions. This explosive metaphor is one that is invited by the book, whose chapters are given titles derived from
the nuclear vocabulary, and whose three major sections are entitled "Fission," "Fusion," and "Critical Mass." An actual explosion
is countered by a metaphorical one, and what that metaphor conveys is the shock of imaginative apprehension.

If this is O'Brien's answer to the question that began his book,
it is an answer of a peculiar kind, one described by Blanchot:

There is the answer to the question, but then too, the answer
that makes the question possible; and also the one that redou-
bles the question, makes it last and does not appease it, but on
the contrary confers upon it a new brilliance, ensures its sharp-
ness—there is the interrogative answer. (1986, 30)

This answer O'Brien has called forth; he has done so through a
structure like that described by Michel Leiris, in metaphors that
evoke both Magritte and Blanchot:

The poetic structure—like a cannon, which is only a hole sur-
rounded by steel—can be based only on what one does not have;
. . . ultimately one can write only to fill a void or at the very

least to situate . . . the place where this incommensurable abyss
yawns within us. (1963, 105)

4

The paradoxes of remembering and forgetting exemplified in
O'Brien's book can only be known *through* such exemplification,
as Augustine once indicated: "Forgetfulness, when we remember
it, is not present to the memory itself, but by its image: because
if it were present by itself, it would not cause us to remember, but
to forget" (cited in Perlman 1988, 178–79). The status of the image, and of the imaginary, is a recurrent theme in Blanchot's
thought, and we are impelled to consider it now by Cowling's (or
O'Brien's) claims about the crucial power of the imagination.

Certainly the image in Blanchot has a power that is crucial
even to the construction of the real to which it is sometimes
opposed: "Only what has surrendered itself to the image appears," he says, "and everything that appears is, in this sense,
imaginary" (1981, 84). What else could it be? What other way
could interpose itself as a way of apprehending that reality we
only know as image? Blanchot resists "the usual analysis" according to which

> the image exists after the object: the image follows from it; we
> see, then we imagine. After the object comes the image. "After"
> means that first the thing must move away in order to allow it-
> self to be grasped again. But that distancing is not the simple
> change of place of a moving object, which nevertheless remains
> the same. Here the distancing is at the heart of the thing. The
> thing was there, we grasped it in the living motion of a compre-
> hensive action—and once it has become an image it instantly be-
> comes ungraspable, noncontemporary, impassive, not the same
> thing distanced, but that thing as distancing, the present thing
> in its absence. (1981, 80–81)

In this sense, the image is certainly not going to help us imagine
a future, at least not in any conventional, comforting sense. Not
an agenda, planned in advance, but an open and interminable

space, the future *is* distancing; always receding, it draws us, fascinated, into it.

We must recognize, however, that this is one of "Two Versions of the Imaginary" described in Blanchot's essay of that name. The "usual analysis" is not rejected, in which "the image becomes the follower of the object, what comes after it, what remains of it and allows us to have it still available to us when nothing is left of it, a great resource, a fecund and judicious power" (1981, 86). If Blanchot resists this version, it is because it is "usual" to the point of excluding its opposite. But Blanchot rejects *neither* version:

> What we have called the two versions of the imaginary, this fact that the image can help us to recapture the thing in an ideal way, being, then, its vitalizing negation, but also, on the level we are drawn to by its own weight, constantly threatening to send us back, no longer to the absent thing, but to absence as presence, to the neutral double of the object, in which belonging to the world has vanished: this duplicity is not such that one can pacify it with an "either, or else," capable of permitting a choice and of taking away from choice the ambiguity that makes it possible. (1981, 88)

The fact that the ambiguity of choice is instated in the space between the two versions of the imaginary reinscribes a quality crucial to the idea of a future: that it is undetermined, either by controlling agendas or by their necessary ruin.

Perhaps we can get a better idea of Blanchot's two versions of the imaginary through yet another version. For all of this talk of imagination (in O'Brien, in Blanchot) encourages us to turn to the romantic period—that other time, besides our own, in which poetics was closely related to apocalypse. Specifically, I want to turn now to the familiar passage in book 6 of *The Prelude* immediately following Wordsworth's realization that the anticipated moment of crossing the Alps has already passed without his knowing it, and without having satisfied that anticipation. What happens then happens in the emptiness beyond the page. When words resume they can describe the experience only in retrospect; and those words have an interesting and uneasy relationship to the words found by Blanchot for the disaster:

> Imagination—here the Power so called
> Through sad incompetence of human speech—
> That awful Power rose from the Mind's abyss
> Like an unfathered vapour that enwraps
> At once some lonely Traveller. I was lost,
> Halted without an effort to break through;
> But to my conscious soul I now can say,
> "I recognize thy glory"; in such strength
> Of usurpation, when the light of sense
> Goes out, but with a flash that has revealed
> The invisible world, doth Greatness make abode,
> There harbours, whether we be young or old;
> Our destiny, our being's heart and home,
> Is with infinitude, and only there;
> With hope it is, hope that can never die,
> Effort, and expectation, and desire,
> And something evermore about to be.
>
> (1985, ll. 592–608)

I would first like to dwell on the image of the "mind's abyss," which is related to Leiris's "incommensurable abyss within us" and to an image that occurs repeatedly in Blanchot. An example: in *The Writing of the Disaster* Blanchot mocks the presumption of theoreticians who assume they are making progress, step by step. Each step, he says, is only another step toward what he ironically calls "the abyss of truth." "Thence," he continues, "rises the silent murmuring, the tacit intensity" (1986, 42). This scene is reminiscent not only of the passage in book 6 but of another in book 14 where Wordsworth on Mount Snowden hears through a rift in the clouds—"a fixed, abysmal, gloomy breathing-place"—the roar of innumerable waters. To Wordsworth this appears as

> the emblem of a Mind
> That feeds upon infinity, that broods
> Over the dark abyss, intent to hear
> Its voices issuing forth to silent light
> In one continuous stream.
> (1985, ll. 70–74)

Something arises from this abyss, then; something comes out of this nothing. In *The Prelude* Wordsworth hails it as "Imagination," even while admitting that this label is inadequate. Its effect is disastrous. "I was lost," Wordsworth tells us, echoing his Alpine experience and through the image of dense mist intensifying the danger of annihilation.

What is lost is the "I"; all sense of self is usurped. Self is displaced by loss, blankness, nothingness. "The light of sense goes out"—but, Wordsworth adds, "with a flash." Here, perhaps, a hint of that explosion spoken of by Blanchot, and of what that explosion signifies: a moment of intense illumination, even if what is illuminated is the void. In Wordsworth the flash reveals "the invisible world" associated with infinitude. That world, he claims, is our home—not, as in Blanchot, what is outside of us. Indeed, even the notion of an outside is falsely comforting if it implies an inside, a closed entity that we can call self or home. That entity is perpetually riven with an abyss, a hole in the self. Levinas expresses it like this:

> To revert to oneself is not to settle oneself at home, even if
> stripped of all one's acquisitions. It is to be like a stranger,
> hunted down even in one's home, contested in one's own identity
> and one's very poverty, which, like a skin still enclosing the
> self, would establish it in an inwardness, already settled on it-
> self, already a substance. (1981, 92)

This somewhat paranoid way of putting it may be extreme, but no less than Wordsworth's comfortable domestication of otherness. And he doesn't stop there. Whether through Wordsworth's relentless optimism, or sheer homologous sound, "home" leads to "hope"—a hope which is asserted but scarcely justified. I do not mean by this to dismiss the notion of hope (indeed one of my main purposes in analyzing the Wordsworth passage is to introduce it), but I will defer to the next chapter the problem of whether hope may be recuperated in a more acceptable version.

The passage from *The Prelude* ends with the triple surges of "Effort, and expectation, and desire, / And something evermore about to be." In his stress on what is "about to be" Wordsworth is, like O'Brien's protagonist, imagining a future—not a specific future so much as the *concept* of a future. And here again he is in opposition to Blanchot, for whom the disaster annihilates all concepts of time, including those of beginning and end. The disaster sucks everything into it, like the vanishing point in a perspective; yet at the same time it is ultimate source and origin—as it is in Wordsworth. In the lines that follow the passage we have been examining he compares the powers of the imagination, in a traditional image, to the fertilizing powers of the overflowing Nile—only the fact that the Nile's source was at that time unknown, hidden, is now linked to the experience just described of personal annihilation. Out of that nothing comes "something"— no more specific words for it can be found, "through sad incompetence of human speech."

It is significant that all this comes to Wordsworth while he is writing *The Prelude,* and *through* the act of writing. This book of *The Prelude,* and indeed the whole of *The Prelude,* here explodes. The passage offers not meaning but an understanding that is beyond words, to whose threshold we may come through words. It may be true, as Blanchot asserts, that any text is empty: "At bottom it doesn't exist; you have to cross an abyss, and if you do not jump, you do not comprehend" (1986, 10). But we do, continually, cross that abyss; and we may retain something of what it gives us. The experience indicated by Wordsworth clearly takes place in the abyss between two moments of writing, in the emptiness of the unwritten page, when the pen drops from the fingers. Blanchot reminds us that what we comprehend in *all* writing arises from the abyss, the emptiness between sentences, between words. Yet even if the ultimate goal of words is to dispense with themselves, the words themselves cannot be dispensed with: "For what escapes all that can be said . . . escapes only under the auspices of Saying and when kept back by the restraint that is Saying's alone" (Blanchot 1986, 114). Our apprehension of the abyss explodes only in a closed chamber, a structure of restraint which intensifies all that force that is beyond restraint and beyond structure. Only under such circumstances can that force be evoked.

That force is of course the disaster. But after what has been said, that metaphor does not seem entirely appropriate. Even Blanchot at one point muses, "Perhaps we know the disaster by other, perhaps joyful names" (1986, 6). For this ultimate effect of literature is not necessarily, like a true disaster, something to be feared and resisted. Fear there may be, and in no one more than the writer, faced with the blankness of a page, which is the continual rebuttal to all words. Yet the writer, inarticulate, somehow finds words to fill the blank abyss; and if they are the right words they will not cover the abyss but manifest it, and evoke that which is beyond articulation. Our responses to what is evoked may encompass complete opposites: "Thus does the patience of the disaster lead us to expect nothing of the 'cosmic' and perhaps nothing of the world, or, on the contrary, very much of the world, if we succeed in disengaging it from the idea of order, or regularity guaranteed by law" (1986, 75). Through the evocation of the abyss, then, something may be affirmed, though not through any single affirmation. No statement emerges from our encounter with the abyss, no political program, no conceptual system, scarcely anything that could be called content. Nevertheless, something is comprehended, exploding in our minds so that, at least momentarily, we approach Otherness. That otherness includes in its spectrum an elusive philosophical concept; the specific incarnation of otherness that we find in the nuclear bomb; and a future that is other than the present in which we try to make our home. On such abysmal realities we build our lives, and we build them through continual imaginative acts. The nuclear explosion that will annihilate imagination can be countered, if not annihilated, by that explosion in the mind which is a metaphor for imagination's disastrous force. Works such as *The Nuclear Age, Fiskadoro,* and *Einstein on the Beach* do not answer, but they affirm. They allow us to return to our lives and, in the very space of disaster, to imagine a future.

Hope of a Tree

Near the conclusion of his essay on "Différance" Derrida strikes a note that is repeated throughout his work: one of Nietzschean affirmation, an affirmation of play, of dance, of laughter. He then goes on to compare Nietzsche's version with another version of affirmation in these words:

> From the vantage of this laughter and this dance, from the vantage of this affirmation foreign to all dialectics, the other side of nostalgia, what I will call Heideggerian *hope,* comes into question. I am not unaware how shocking this word might seem here. Nevertheless I am venturing it, without excluding any of its implications. (1982, 26)

Yet Derrida, it turns out, is opening himself to this concept only so that he may deconstruct it, putting into question and excluding every one of its implications. Hope comes into question—but into a particular form of the question, which here is not Heideggerian but Derridean. So if an acceptable answer to the question of hope is to be arrived at—which is what I hope to do here—it will have to be done by way of a detour, considering to begin with the terms that for Derrida create obstacles.

"The question" is restated in Derrida's next paragraph, implying something like a definition of hope, or perhaps merely Derrida's idea of what is hoped for in logocentric thinking: "Such is the question: the alliance of speech and Being in the unique word, in the finally proper name." This version of Heideggerian hope has emerged from Derrida's reading of the following passage in Heidegger's "Anaximander Fragment."

> In order to name the essential nature of Being, language would have to find a single word, the unique word. From this we can gather how daring every thoughtful word addressed to Being is. Nevertheless such daring is not impossible, since Being speaks always and everywhere through language. (1975, 52)

Derrida's rebuttal to this passage takes the form of slowing down the last sentence, putting it into question, in his final words, by putting it up against the *différance* that has been his subject throughout.

> And such is the question inscribed in the simulated affirmation of *différance*. It bears (on) each member of this sentence: "Being/ speaks/ always and everywhere/ throughout/ language."

Certainly anyone who is familiar with Derrida's thinking can see how every part of this sentence involves a heresy. But by considering the sentence in parts as he does, doesn't Derrida address himself to the "unique word," or to a series of unique words, isolated for scrutiny of their essence or lack of essence? Whereas the sentence can be read (indeed must be read if it is to be a sentence at all) with an attention that hovers over the whole—a whole that is smaller than language, but that like language requires a movement that is "always and everywhere throughout." This movement, we may find, is not so different from Derrida's "play which makes possible nominal effects, the relatively unitary and atomic structures that are called names" (1982, 26). A name like Being, then, can take its meaning only in the volatile play of other names.

It is Heidegger's project in "The Anaximander Fragment" to recover the name of Being as it is spoken in the earliest existing fragment of Western thinking, dating from the early sixth century B.C. He does this not out of veneration for the ancient, or a

search for origins, but in order to go beyond the origins of meta-
physics in Plato and Aristotle to hear the name of Being anew
and to remember what has been systematically forgotten. His
procedure is painstakingly philological; but even when he is calling upon Greek etymologies, Heidegger remains aware that no
unique word has meaning except through the play with other
words. All of these words must first of all be attained through
translation in an unusual sense: "Our thinking must first, before
translating, be translated to what is said in Greek" (1975, 19).
This sort of paradoxical translation (we must know what the
sentence says before we can read it) might be expected to be ap-
pealing to Derrida, but it does not seem to have been practiced in
his "translation" of the Heidegger fragment. His reading criticizes above all a privileging of presence, a return of the "metaphysical" in the midst of Heidegger's antimetaphysical project.
But Derrida chooses to forget Heidegger's earlier arguments,
which remind us of the paradoxical Greek twinning of presence
and absence:

> In Greek experience what comes to presence remains ambigu-
> ous, and indeed necessarily so. . . . Presencing preserves in un-
> concealment what is present both at the present time and not at
> the present time. . . . As protection of Being, preservation be-
> longs to the herdsman, who has so little to do with bucolic
> idylls and Nature mysticism that he can be the herdsman of
> Being only if he continues to hold the place of nothingness.
> Both are the Same. (1975, 35, 36)

The "early sign" of Being, according to Heidegger, is Truth or
Aletheia—a word that contains within it the abyssal river of
Lethe. Truth is not so much a revelation as a nonforgetting—an
"unconcealment" marks the place of being, which is also the
place of nothingness. When we speak of being speaking, then, we
must also speak of nothingness speaking always and everywhere
throughout language. But why should this be so?

Blanchot now gives us the best way to continue our detour and bring it to an end: he allows us to shift the site of our questions back to literature, and eventually to circle back to the question that put into motion all these others, the question of hope.

For Blanchot, language is fundamentally ambiguous, partaking of both being and death in a way that might recall Heidegger's pairing of the two if it were not explicitly referred to Hegel. A fragment from an early essay of Hegel's states that "Adam's first act, which made him master of the animals, was to give them names, that is, he annihilated them in their existence (as existing creatures)." In his essay on "Literature and the Right to Death" Blanchot comments:

> Hegel means that from that moment on the cat ceased to be a uniquely real cat and became an idea as well. The meaning of speech, then, requires that before any word is spoken there must be a sort of immense hecatomb, a preliminary flood plunging all of creation into a total sea. God had created living creatures, but man had to annihilate them. Not until then did they take on meaning for him, and he in turn created them out of the death into which they had disappeared; only instead of beings (*êtres*) and, as we say, existants (*existants*), there remained only being (*l'être*). (1981, 42)

And this process does not stop, cannot stop with a unique word: the annihilation that in the beginning gave rise to the word speaks throughout language. Indeed, it is only through the "throughout" that it speaks at all, insofar as language composes itself out of differences. And when it speaks presence it also speaks the absence that created presence, the death that created the concept of being. Yet this death is not the final word. No word can sum up the nature of any one word, or of the language it pulls with it into an abyss where is found neither being nor nothingness but an ambiguity akin to *différance*. It is literature that enacts most vividly this ambiguity, this "strange slipping back and forth between being and not being, presence and absence, reality and nonreality" (1981, 57). And this is not the end of hope any more than it is its beginning.

A literary text indeed deconstructs itself or perhaps explodes—but the effect that act may have is as ambiguous as the text itself.

> This instability can appear to be the effect of a disintegrating force, since it can cause the strongest, most forceful work to become a work of unhappiness and ruin, but this disintegration is also a form of construction, if it suddenly causes distress to turn to hope and destruction into an element of the indestructible. (1981, 60–61)

At the close of his essay, Blanchot sums up this double meaning:

> Death ends in being: this is man's hope and his task, because nothingness itself helps to make the world, nothingness is the creator of the world in man as he works and understands. Death ends in being: this is man's laceration, the source of his unhappy fate, since by man death comes to being and by man meaning rests on nothingness. (1981, 62)

What Blanchot presents us with here is a choice, and this is itself an affirmation; for choice, as we have seen, is a condition for imagining a future. As is motion. Thus choice is not a resting point to be decided upon but the restless openness of alternatives, a circling that is perhaps vicious or perhaps generative of a certain kind of power:

> This ultimate vicissitude keeps the work in suspense in such a way that it can choose whether to take on a positive or a negative value and, as though it were pivoting invisibly around an invisible axis, enter the daylight of affirmations or the backlight of negations. (1981, 60)

As the work can choose between positive and negative values, so can we: the work chooses through us, perhaps chooses us. And we in turn can choose whether to make its choices our own—choices that may extend from the theoretical being and/or nothingness of a text to the "fabulous textuality" of nuclear war and all that is constructed from it in the material world. And when we make our choice—no matter what that choice may be—we always do so in the expectation of some gain to ourselves, even though the form of this expected gain may sometimes be highly indirect and psychologically convoluted. That expectation is a variety of hope: where choices are made they must be made in hope. I choose then to turn back to this hoary old concept in the hope that it may yet have something new to say to us.

1

Heideggerian hope has been described by Derrida as "the other side of nostalgia." Let us accept that description and pursue its ramifications in another work that centers around the nuclear question, this time a film. For the Russian filmmaker Andrey Tarkovsky nostalgia is a key concept—indeed *Nostalgia* is the title of one of his films. Nostalgia may even be the essence of film: "Cinema lives by its capacity to resurrect the same event on the screen time after time—by its very essence it is, so to speak, *nostalgic*" (Tarkovsky 1986, 140). Thus his 1986 nuclear film *The Sacrifice* is an exploration of various senses of this concept— return, repetition, resurrection—an exploration that finally takes us to that other side of nostalgia, hope.

Near the beginning of *The Sacrifice* hope is invoked only to be lost. It is a postman who speaks:

> We hope. We wait for something. We hope, we lose hope, we move closer to death. Finally we die and are born again. But we remember nothing. . . . And then everything begins again from scratch. Not literally the same way, just a wee, wee bit different. But it's still so hopeless . . . and we don't know why.

On a remote shore in Sweden Otto the postman has bicycled out to deliver a birthday telegram to Alexander, a one-time actor who is now a theater critic of some reputation. Perhaps because the day is one that marks time in Alexander's life, and does so by returning, the two men fall into a philosophical discussion cen- tering particularly on Nietzsche's concept of eternal return. In Nietzsche that concept is affirmative, a world without end that is

solely of this earth. This kind of eternity is not a tyrannical instrument of deferred reward or punishment, but a moral weight
upon one's actions (the unbearable heaviness of being) that arises
from the actions themselves, destined to be repeated endlessly.
This endless repetition can evoke a sense of futility and horror,
as it does with Otto the postman.

But the concept of a return itself returns later in the film as
something to be wished for, prayed for. Even as Alexander's
birthday celebration takes place, the television goes dead, the
thunder of missiles passes overhead, the power fails, and the
little group is left awaiting its fate. Little Man, the son of Alexander's old age, has mercifully been put to bed earlier in the eve-
ning. After looking in on him Alexander prays, promising to God
a comprehensive sacrifice:

> I will give Thee all that I have.
> I'll give up my family, whom I love.
> I'll destroy my home, and give up Little Man.
> I'll be mute and never speak another word to anyone.
> I will relinquish everything that binds me to life, if only Thou
> dost restore everything as it was before, as it was this morning,
> and yesterday.

The terms that Alexander has offered God are significant. What
he is ultimately sacrificing is self, the self that was being cele-
brated by his birthday, and the self that we learn in the first part
of the film has been established by excluding all that Alexander
must now learn to include.

Once an actor, Alexander is now a theater critic: a man of
words, whose words are an act of possession and control. As
Alexander explains why he gave up a successful acting career, it
becomes apparent that his main need was the ego's need to control: "An actor's identity dissolves in his roles. I didn't want my
ego dissolved. There was something in it that struck me as sin-
ful, something feminine and weak." (That women are not exempt
from this attitude is demonstrated by Alexander's wife Adelaide,

whose egoism is even more tragically irrevocable than his: despite being an actress, she confesses that she has always said to herself, "Don't give in to anything or you'll die.") For these reasons Alexander has abdicated from acting, and from his most famous role as Prince Myshkin, from fool and saint and sacrificed ego to that which words seemed to offer him: a self. It is that self which he now promises to sacrifice.

Before Alexander's promises can be accepted, one more sacrifice is asked of him: he must fly in the face of what is controlled and reasonable, he must become a fool. Tapping on Alexander's window, Otto awakens him. He tells Alexander that his only chance is his housekeeper Maria, whom Otto has "documented" as a witch, one powerful enough to reverse the world's destiny. He must go to her, seek out the feminine that he had sought to purge, and sleep with her. Understandably, Alexander hesitates, but he finally takes Otto's bicycle and makes his way to Maria's farmhouse. The encounter there is equivocal, but Maria is touched enough by his desperation to relent. And when Alexander wakes the next morning in his room, it is again the morning of his birthday, and the world is as it was. He proceeds to fulfill his promise. Clad in his black kimono, limping from a bad knock, he methodically sets fire to his house while its occupants are on a walk. As they come running back, Alexander begins to blurt out his confession and then remembers his promise, instantly becoming mute. He is taken away in an ambulance as a madman, an idiot.

The translation to muteness is the most significant turnaround for Alexander and indeed for the whole film. *The Sacrifice* has begun with a scene whose visual barrenness is played against an uninterrupted flow of words for the first half hour of the film. Most of these words come from Alexander, and they are addressed to Little Man. The child answers nothing, for he has had an operation on his throat, which is bandaged, and he is under orders not to talk. When Otto joins them, more words follow, and after the postman wobbles off on his bicycle, Alexander continues his monologue—though with signs of impatience even toward his son. "'In the beginning was the word,'" he quotes, "but you are mute, mute as a fish." He concludes with an outburst: "God, how weary I am of this talk! If only someone would stop talking and *do* something instead. Or at least try to." Out of the silence that follows this, Little Man does something— launches himself bodily on his father in a surprise attack. Over-shooting the mark, he tumbles into the grass and raises himself with blood on his face. The sight of him triggers a strange faint-ing fit in his father, accompanied by a wordless vision.

In black and white, a deserted street. Papers and rubbish lit-ter it and drift through the air. An abandoned stool, the over-turned wreck of a car, streams of water, refuse everywhere—un-til the moving camera passes over a spattered pane of glass in which are reflected the facades of houses against the sky. This pane of glass may be compared to the one that covers the "terri-fying" image of Leonardo's *Adoration of the Three Kings* which hangs in Alexander's bedroom. Peering at it later in the film Otto says, "I can't see clearly. It's behind a pane of glass, and it's so dark." The connection to Paul's letter to the Corinthians is almost too evident. In both moments of the film it is the glass's tendency to act as a mirror which obscures the mystery behind it; in the case of the Leonardo, its glass mirrors the faces of Otto and Alexander. What is glimpsed, however briefly, is a reality beyond the one that mirrors back the public facade, the public face—the constructed identity that, according to Lacan, was initiated by the mirror image. But Alexander's visionary image is on the "other side" of the glass; insofar as it goes beyond the mirror it goes beyond ego, the ego that is constructed with words and sees itself in them.

The move from word to image is a dramatization of Tar-kovsky's own theoretical position. With all the militance of a com-mitted filmmaker, he announces, "The time has come for litera-ture to be separated, once and for all, from cinema" (Tarkovsky 1986, 15). Admitting that the two exercise "a strong and beneficial influence on each other" (1986, 22), Tarkovsky yet finds irreconcilable differences, stemming from the essential disparity between word and screened image. In any film, admittedly, there is a literary element; but that element is "smelted," says Tarkovsky; "it ceases to be literature once the film is made" (1986, 134). In this particular film that process becomes part of the film's overt content. Words stand for a certain element in humanity which must be evoked *in order* to be sacrificed. They become a burnt offering, a holocaust to counter the nuclear one. Robert Frost once compared the motion of a poem to ice sliding across a hot stove: it is only through the process of consuming itself that a poem can move, in any sense. The hot stove in Tarkovsky's film is nuclear holocaust, which provides the impetus for Alexander's sacrifice.

Where ego was, image shall be, in a turning back of the process that created the ego in the first place. And in Tarkovsky's view of the matter, image takes on almost mystical properties: it is "a hieroglyphic of absolute truth . . . *sui generis* detector of the absolute. Through the image is sustained an awareness of the infinite: the eternal within the finite, the spiritual within matter, the limitless given form" (1986, 37). This sort of rhetoric reflects the spirituality that causes Tarkovsky to use orthodox Christian references in his films, while at the same time being far from orthodox. Indeed, he practices rather better than he preaches. His notion of the image is not so "absolute" that it is characterized by an ontotheological stability; it is as shifting and ambiguous as Blanchot's notion. And, as will become evident, it has less to do with eternity than with time.

We must first understand that the above description of the image does not refer to one which is static, the "shot." Tarkovsky resists "structuralist attempts to look at a frame as a sign of something else, the meaning of which is summed up in the shot" (1986, 177). The hieroglyphic of the image is not to be taken as a signifier, like the word. A word "is itself an idea, a concept, to some extent an abstraction." In contrast, a cinema frame "is always a particle of reality, bearing no idea; only the film as a whole could be said to carry . . . an ideological version of reality" (1986, 177). The idea of the image expands, then, to comprehend the coherence of the entire work. Tarkovsky distinguishes his idea of image from Eisenstein's idea of montage as the fundamental principle of cinema: montage is too much a self-conscious language for Tarkovsky's taste, too literary. Likewise he separates himself from those who argue that the editing of a film is paramount because the film's effect is made through its rhythm. "Rhythm is determined not by the length of the edited pieces, but by the time that runs through them," he says (1986, 117). In this latter sense rhythm, not editing, is crucial to the idea of the image: "The dominant, all-powerful factor of the film image is *rhythm,* expressing the course of time within the frame" (1986, 113).

But we are within the frame again, when just before this Tarkovsky was resisting attempts to define the image in terms of a single shot. The discrepancy may be resolved in the realization that for Tarkovsky *the idea of the cinematic image is not so much pictorial as it is temporal.* If this is so, the course of time may be felt within the individual shot as well as in the aggregate of shots which makes up the film as a whole. For this reason Tarkovsky heads off any effort by his actors to "build up" a character, to adopt a "method," to see the moment they are acting as part of a larger whole. In an extreme case like that of Margarita Trekhova in *Mirror,* he did not even allow an actress to know the outcome of the character's situation: "Within the given framework of waiting for her husband, the actress had to live out her own *mysterious* fragment of life ignorant of where it might be leading" (1986, 141). That her life is mysterious is stressed in this sentence as it is in the screen image, where the felt pressure, the rhythm, of a real temporal experience conveys its strivings beyond the finite present.

There are ways of underscoring this mysterious aspect of the image, but these must never be impressed *upon* the temporal unit. Rather the mysteriousness of time must be allowed to manifest itself through an art of subtraction. Significantly, Tarkovsky's "reflections on the cinema" were entitled by him *Sculpting in Time*. The film director, like a sculptor, removes from time what is superfluous to the emerging image. Consequently, Tarkovsky's common (though not inevitable) fondness for stark and barren decor; his wistful desire to work in black and white rather than in color; the slow pace of many scenes, evoking a counterpressure in the viewer akin to yearning; his use of silences and music. In *The Sacrifice,* for instance, the music—traditional Swedish shepherds' calls—literally evokes vast distances, fragmented attempts at connection, communication that is other than that of words: "The spirit hears the echo of the *otherwise*" (Levinas 1981, 44). Such techniques free the viewers and allow them to feel, if they will, the quality of time aspiring beyond itself. In one sense this is an "illusion," as Tarkovsky has said; in another sense it is real to the degree that the image is a block of real time, whose movement beyond itself defines it as temporal.

This aspect of the moment in time is manifested in the very form that apparently attempts to counter it, that species of return that is repetition. If we return here to Kierkegaard's statement on repetition, cited earlier, we see in it a link to that species of return called nostalgia, as well as a distinction from it: "Repetition and recollection are the same movement, only in opposite directions; for what is recollected has been, is repeated backwards, whereas repetition properly so called is recollected forwards" (1964, 53). Under the guise of being the same, repetition can never return to itself. Subtracting all extraneous change, repetition foregrounds the fact of pure change, the fact of time as an "astonishing divergence of the identical from itself," as Levinas has put it (1981, 44). Paradoxically what is produced by a return to the same is a subtle sense of difference. That sense, because of its links to change, is "recollected forwards"; it is impelled toward the future rather than the past. And to the degree that it moves toward a future this version of return is characterized by the possibility of hope.

Let us now turn back to Nietzsche's eternal return, and to Otto the postman's sense of hopelessness about it. At one point in *The Sacrifice* he expresses this sense with an example: "Here comes a cockroach running around a plate. He fancies he's moving forward with a definite purpose." But Otto is interrupted by an objection: "How do you know what a cockroach thinks? It could be a ritual." This adds another term to the complex of ideas around the concept of return, and perhaps the most important one.

A ritual is often made up of the most mundane sort of action, one that is habitually repeated—only now it is slowed, played through with a heightened awareness, until this piece of time evokes something beyond itself; an example is the Japanese tea ceremony. "In a sense," Tarkovsky has observed, "the Japanese could be said to be trying to master time as the stuff of art" (1986, 57). It may be significant, then, that there is a persistent Japanese motif throughout *The Sacrifice:* Alexander dons a black kimono before setting fire to his home; his stereo plays traditional Japanese flute music; the dry stick planted at the film's opening is called an "ikebana" in the original narrative.

In this opening Alexander and Little Man are planting a dead tree, little more than a branched stick, on the shore. Meanwhile, Alexander tells his son the story of a disciple who was directed by his master to plant a stick and to water it every day until it came to life. After painfully carrying a bucket of water to the spot every day for three years, the disciple arrived one morning to find that the tree was covered in blossoms. "If every single day at exactly the same stroke of the clock," Alexander then says, "one were to perform the same single action, like a ritual . . . the world would be changed."

Return then leads to change, not just to more of the same. Alexander gets his wish for the world to be "as it was before, as it was this morning and yesterday." But though the time is identical, everything else is changed. In his brief essay on *The Sacrifice* (1987), Tarkovsky stresses that at the film's end *everything* is different from what it was before. The changes have affected not only Alexander but also characters such as Adelaide, and beyond this little group the unseen mass of humanity, which now too has some hope of change. Little as it is, the group can serve as a model—like the model of his house that Alexander finds on the ground and that Otto has helped his son to make as a birthday gift. Tarkovsky's film is another such model, a model of return.

Not only *The Sacrifice* but Tarkovsky's entire film oeuvre is inextricably related to return. The film image itself returns, is resurrected time after time. Frame after frame passes by in repetition, to all appearances the same; yet something is changing, something moves on the screen. And this moving in turn may move the viewer and give rise to a change that Tarkovsky has again described in terms of return. He speaks of "how time in its moral implication is in fact turned back" (1986, 58). The source of any action, of any moral decision, is always anterior to it, he argues. In that sense "we could be said to be turning time back through conscience" (1986, 59). For Tarkovsky an important purpose of art is this turning back: the great works of art "stand on man's path like ciphers of catastrophe, announcing 'Danger! No entry!' They range themselves at the sites of possible or impending cataclysms, like warning signs at the edges of precipices or quagmires" (1986, 53). Yet if this is to be done, the artist must not turn back from the abyss: "Artistic creation demands of the artist that he 'perish utterly,' in the full, tragic sense of those words," writes Tarkovsky (1986, 39), who in fact was dying at the time that he directed *The Sacrifice*. The turning back that can be produced by artistic creation is a return from a "dessicated" state: Tarkovsky uses the word to refer both to the stick planted by Alexander, and to the entire current state of Western civilization.

The ambulance that is taking Alexander away at the end of
The Sacrifice passes by the planted stick of the film's opening, to
which Little Man is lugging a bucket of water. He empties it; lies
beneath the tree, gazing up at the dry branches; then speaks for
the first time in the film. He recollects his father's words about
the word: "'In the beginning was the word.' Why is that, Papa?"
he asks. Whatever we take the child's question to mean, it is
casting doubt upon the primacy of the word, the same word that
has been relinquished by the father for the sake of his son.

The camera moves up the tree's trunk and holds at its dry
branches, viewed against the waters of the bay. Here at the end of
The Sacrifice it is time to return to the eternal task of creating a
future in time. So on the threshold of the "absolute" (which is to
say at the moment of the fulfilled cinematic image), Tarkovsky
turns to time, this time, and to his own son who will live on after
Tarkovsky has crossed the threshold of his death. Over the image
of the tree shimmering with reflected light—an image both barren and rich—are superimposed these words:

> THIS FILM IS DEDICATED TO MY SON ANDREY
> IN TRUST AND HOPE

2

The allusion in the final image of *The Sacrifice* is to Job 14:7–9:

> For there is hope of a tree, if it be cut down, that it will sprout
> again, and that the tender branch thereof will not cease.
> Though the root thereof wax old in the earth, and the stock
> thereof die in the ground; yet through the scent of water it will
> bud, and bring forth boughs like a plant.

Unexpectedly, this passage appears in *Riddley Walker,* trans-
muted thus:

> Which theres hoap of a tree if its cut down yet itwl sprout agen.
> And them tinder branches theyre of wil not seaze. Tho the root
> of it works old in the earf and the stick of it dead on the groun

yet even jus only the smel of water and itwl bud and bring forit
bowing like the plan. (1982, 170)

Orfing, the former second in command of Inland's government,
explains that this has been the "go word" of the opposition, one
that has been passed down year after year. That opposition has
now finally triumphed: Goodparley, the Pry Mincer, hangs help-
less in torture to make him reveal his secrets. Riddley, witness-
ing this, understands the meaning of a curious piece of graffiti
he has found earlier above the words HOAP OF A TREE:

> On a wall some bodyd drawt some thing with a bit of chard coal.
> What it wer it wer a joak picter of Goodparley. Rough done but
> you cud see it wer him easy a nuff. With his littl eyes and big
> chin and big teef he wer easy to do. Coming out of each side of
> his mouf wer vines and leaves. (1982, 164)

Yet the origins of this image, like those of the words, extend
beyond their cooptation by the opposition movement, and the
meaning they have there.

The image first appears to Riddley as he stands in the crypt of
"stoan trees" that is the womb of Cambry. It appears in his mind's
eye with astonishing clarity:

> I knowit that dint come out of my mynd it musve come in to it
> from somers. Where ever that mans face come from it fult me
> sad. It wer a thick kynd of face. Thick nose lookit like it ben
> bustit. Thick mouf ½ open and the leafy vines growing out of
> boath sides and curling up roun his head. Lookit like he myt be
> wearing a hood as wel. The way his mouf wer open and how his
> eyes lookit it wer like he dint know what to make of it. Like he
> ben breaving and suddn the breaf coming out of his mouf ternt
> in to vines and leaves. Cudnt swaller them back and tryd to bite
> them off but theyre too hard and thick and pulling his mouf a
> part wider all the time. His eyes wide open with sir prize. Lite
> green eyes open so wide. (1982, 160)

After the vivid detail in which he has realized this image in his
mind, it does not surprise Riddley at all when the dog pack

leads him to a stone under which is something wrapped in cloth; even before unwrapping the package he knows he will find Greanvine, as he has named the face in his mind. It is carved out of wood, there is a broken peg in back, and it has the feel of great age.

The face Riddley finds is that of the so-called Green Man, a common motif in medieval architecture, as well as in stained glass, illuminated manuscripts, and paintings. Studies of the Green Man's meaning usually come to no conclusion about that meaning. According to Kathleen Basford, for instance, it is a "dynamic image, capable of infinite expansion," one which "could not only stimulate but deeply disturb the imagination" (1978, 21). Such is its effect in Russell Hoban's novel, for any interpretation soon branches out into another. This is exemplified when Riddley changes the image scrawled on the wall to make it correspond to his way of seeing it:

> Goodparley had a long chin and the chin in the picter wer even longer. At the top of that long chin the vines and leaves coming out of the mouf lookit like stag horns and the long chin lookit like the stags head. There ben a bit of chard coal lef on the floor I pickt it up and drawit in the stags eyes and nose and ears. There wer Goodparley in be twean the horns of the Hart of the Wud then. Unner neath of it the words:
>
> HOAP OF A TREE
>
> What kynd of a tree wud that be then? (1982, 165)

The Hart of the Wud is of course where the Littl Shynin Man the Addom is found. But I will pass by for now, as Riddley does, the question of what would make up a nuclear tree. Instead I want to underscore the similarity between Riddley's restructuring activity and Derrida's in *The Post Card*. The ambiguous image on the Bodleian post card gives rise to some playful speculations on Derrida's part: Plato is shoving through the back of the chair a massive phallus, which emerges under Socrates' leg; he is taking Socrates out for an excursion in a wheel chair; he is pushing off on a skateboard. At one point Derrida mails out the card with certain (unspecified) alterations that involve cutting and pasting. All this play contributes to a serious argument about deconstructive play, the destabilizing of a centered significance. In *Riddley Walker,* too, the multiple interpretations of Greanvine (linked to still more multiplicities in regard to other images) call into question expectations of understanding and mastery.

Orfing's interpretation, then, linked to mastery as it is, is already inadequate even before he speaks it. Another inadequate interpretation is that of Punch, although we can learn more from that inadequacy. In a sense Greanvine *is* Punch: "Take a way the vines and leaves and it myt be Punchs face" (1982, 160). To be sure, Riddley realizes in the next moment, it could be anyone's face: "I begun to see it wer the onlyes face there wer. It wer every face" (1982, 161). Yet the play between Punch and Greanvine seems to sum up what is at stake, and it is enacted literally as a puppet play by Riddley, Punch on one hand and Greanvine on the other. No conclusion is reached in this dialogue, though Punch does come up with an interpretation that arises straight out of his cocky personality:

> Punch said, 'I am the balls of the worl I am the stoans of the worl. I am the stoans and I have my littl stick.'
> Greanvine said, 'Is that your tree then is that your living wood?'
> Punch said, 'Yes thats what it is its that same and very wood what never dys.' (1982, 167)

The tree he puts his hope in is, then, a phallic tree. But when we recall how the phallus is undercut in other works we have dealt with, we see a new way in which Greanvine may be interpreted. It begins with a curious statement made by Riddley as he first stares at the unwrapped face of Greanvine:

> This wernt a woman thing. A woman in this place by the woom of her what has her woom in Cambry wuntve bothert hiding a

way this face of a man with vines and leaves growing out of his mouf. This here man dying back in to the earf and the vines growing up thru his arse hoal up thru his gullit and out of his mouf. Not a woman thing. Becaws a woman is a *wooma*n aint she. Shes the 1 with the woom shes the 1 with the new life coming out of her. You wunt carve a womans face with vines and leaves growing out of the mouf. (1982, 163)

Whether one agrees with Riddley here depends on how one interprets those vines and leaves. Do they remind us of our necessary dying back into the earth, or are they a sign of new life? If the latter, they would seem entirely appropriate to one who has new life coming out of her—or perhaps they are superfluous, redundant. Perhaps it is men who need to be reminded, by the image of a hole at their center, of that ambiguous space from which arise all possible meanings, which we choose to classify with death or life, being or nothingness. Thus Riddley, upon first seeing the face of Greanvine in his mind, feels something else inside him as well: "I cud feal some thing growing in me it wer like a grean sea surging in me it wer saying, LOSE IT. Saying, LET GO. Saying, THE ONLYES POWER IS NO POWER" (1982, 162).

As a result he does let go: lets go of his earlier exhilarated commitment to recapturing the power of the time before Bad Time. This change comes about as a result of a force in him which Riddley describes as a "grean sea," without realizing that it could just as well be described in such a way as to make himself into the very image he is contemplating. The process of contemplation, growth and branching of thought, breaks its containment in the head, breaks the individual face to powerfully reveal the force of no-power. This green thought, colored by the hope that is its capacity to change that which thinks it, or that which it thinks—this too is hope of a tree. Yet this hope is not smugly comforting; it involves death as well as life, and at least as much loss as gain. The eyes of Greanvine, wide with surprise and possibly even terror, indicate that this hope befalls him like a disaster.

We are returned, then, by way of Blanchot's disaster to the space of literature. That the foliage sprouts only out of the mouth of this Green Man (for other variations are possible) indicates a speaking, though one that is beyond words. The face is mute yet eloquent: "The look of that face saying so many diffrent things only no words to say them with" (1982, 160). Still, words can evoke that which is beyond them, for by that also they exist. The space of that "that" is indeterminable yet hovers throughout language. As the uniqueness of words fissures, revealing their stability to be composed of play, their identity of difference, their being of nothingness, something arises out of that nothing, unfurling, branching. Language's proper self, in shattering, echoes with the unspeakable. So that any writer may say with Job (though perhaps in different accents), "I have uttered that I understood not."

3

"The wish builds up and creates the real, we alone are the gardners of the most mysterious tree, which must grow." So writes Ernst Bloch in 1918 in *The Spirit of Utopia*. Forty years later he quotes himself in a progression of quotations at the end of his monumental three-volume work, *The Principle of Hope*. And his comments—"better thus," "correct thus"—indicate a progression and a growth in his lifetime's work, which of course is far from finished: like Tarkovsky, Bloch dedicates his work to his son. Philosophy itself must grow, he claims. It has heretofore been knowledge obtained from the back, from what was past, as only this could be contemplated. Since Marx, however, there is the chance, indeed the necessity, for philosophy to reverse its direction: "Philosophy will have conscience of tomorrow, commitment to the future, knowledge of hope, or it will have no more knowledge" (1986, 7).

Knowledge of hope is not diffuse or sentimental, as some might expect. To be sure, hope is an emotion: but it is "one of the most exact emotions above every word; because it is not very

changeable, but very characteristic in its intention, and above all
. . . capable of logical and concrete correction and sharpening"
(Bloch 1986, 112). Unchangeable in its own cognitive shape, it is
the prime instrument of change, helping to bring into being a
new real whenever the material conditions are right for its appearance. Of course, wishing is not enough to make it so, but
without the wish—or rather its stronger version, hope—the material world will never even enter into negotiation with human
desire, a negotiation that is necessary if both humanity and the
material world are to develop that in them which is unrealized
and potential.

That Bloch's unorthodox Marxism is concerned with human
realization, the making real of our humanity, does not mean that
he is reinstating *humanism*—not if by that word we mean, as
Derrida does, the dream of full presence, the "reassuring founda-
tion." Quite the contrary. Humanity for Bloch is precisely that
which is not present, the quality of fruitful nonpresence. He
archly defines humanity as "that which still has much before it"
(1986, 245). And this definition would apply, I suspect, not only
to the unfinished state of humanity's history but to any individual human's present sense of being. That present is characterized
by an *expectancy* of future; even when the past is contemplated,
this is done in anticipation of future benefits, or for the benefit of
a future. And that which constantly imagines a future, and by
imagining it becomes a force in its coming to be, is hope.

Yet we may ask how this coming to be itself comes to be. What
is the nature of the temporality out of which a future arises? And
how does the Now become the New? In the rather abstract "Foun-
dation" of *The Principle of Hope* Bloch characterizes the Now as
an always unknowable zero, "the zero of the immediate That of
existing" (1986, 307), a blind spot at the center of lived experience. Contemplating landscape painting, Bloch asks quite simply, "Where does the landscape begin?" For even within the
framed and controlled work of art Bloch notes the tendency of
the foreground to be blurred and without definition in compari-

son to that which takes shape further away. Thus "Not-there is the condition of the Now, and even the Here of this Not-there forms a *zone of silence in the very place where the music is being played*" (1986, 295). Later in *The Principle of Hope,* in the copious examples with which Bloch develops his thinking, this metaphor is reversed: an analysis of sonata and fugue concludes that the real subject of this music is "the hollow space" within it, a space that in his reading of the Syrinx myth Bloch has suggested is the very space of music itself. Real music may partake of the disturbing nature of the sirens' song. So minimalist repetitions may enact the most inaccessible aspects of the Now, of its very inaccessibility: "the moments still beat unheard, unseen, their *present* is at best in the forecourt *of its presence which is not yet conscious, which has not yet become*" (1986, 295). The formulation of a presence that has not yet become, is not present, and yet has presence—all this echoes Heidegger's paradoxical formulations in "The Anaximander Fragment." But for Bloch the most important thing is that this "not yet become" has a drive to become, the "search of the core for its fruit" (1986, 308). The Now is darkness, silence, hollowness perhaps—but not emptiness. A kind of *horror vacui* impels it towards change.

So Bloch takes pains to distinguish between the Not found in the Now and the Nothing that might be confused with it:

> The That in the Now is hollow, is only undefined to begin with, a fermenting *Not.* The Not with which everything starts up and begins, around which every Something is still built. The Not is not there, but because it is thus the Not of a There, it is not simply Not, but at the same time the Not-there. As such the Not cannot bear the presence of itself, is instead related in a driving way to the There of a Something. . . . Because the Not is the beginning of every movement towards something, it is precisely for this reason by no means a Nothing. Instead: Not and Nothing must first be kept as far apart as possible; the whole adventure of definition lies between them. (1986, 306)

The definition Bloch speaks of here is not just the abstract defining of terms, but the gradual coming into definiteness of these terms as they are lived in time. So Bloch suggests a progression from the Not, to the Not-Yet, to the latent end that is literally All or Nothing.

Even in the realization of the "definitivum" that Bloch calls All, there is along the way a positive role to be played by the negativity of Nothing. Unlike the Not, with its drive to break out of itself, the Nothing is pure annihilation. If we ask, with Lear's Fool, "Can you make no use of nothing?" we find that we can. For there is that which should be annihilated, if only to create a space for the Not to fill. So the use of Nothing is, according to Bloch, "annihilation of inadequate Becomeness by immanent explosion" (1986, 310). He explains more fully:

> The Not as *mere Not-Yet alone* could both subjectively and objectively only in fact unsettle inadequate Becomeness, it could not immanently explode it in the way we have described. Explosion is annihilation: and the act of annihilating by definition and by nature is only obtainable from the circulating *Nothing.* The Not seeking its All thus also enters . . . *into a connection with the Nothing, as well as having one with the All.* (1986, 309)

Yet Bloch's militant optimism does not ignore the possibility, beyond such locally useful explosions, of an ultimately explosive end, "the still hypothetically possible *Definitivum of a Nothing"* (1986, 312).

The alternate definitivum, the All, is repeatedly described by Bloch as "homeland." He expresses the exemplary form of this homeland, that which makes it home, as: "harmony of the unreified object with the manifested subject, of the unreified subject with the manifested object" (1986, 248). All of this seems, up to a point, Romantic. It may explain why, in Wordsworth's *Prelude,* home is related to hope. And we may also understand in a new way why that home is found by Wordsworth only through being lost, through an explosive flash: Nothing is incorporated in a process that is optimistic precisely to the degree that it *is process,* that it is "Effort, and expectation, and desire, / And something evermore about to be." Yet Bloch is not simply, as he is sometimes accused of being, a Neo-Romantic; distinctions can be drawn between his ideas of hope and Wordsworth's. For one, Wordsworth is doubtless too enamored of infinitude for Bloch's Marxist purposes. "Something *evermore* about to be" is Bloch's idea of hell: "Nothing is more repugnant to utopian conscience itself than utopia with unlimited travel; endless striving is vertigo, hell" (1986, 314). So he criticizes Bergson for glorifying change in itself, without the directing force that hope can give to change, and that demands objective realization in the world. "The essential content of hope is not hope," he reminds us (1986, 315); it is a concrete goal attained not only by emotion but by objective process in the world. Accordingly a large portion of Bloch's philosophy is devoted to a theory of objects and of their various modes of possibility. A flash of subjective insight is not enough: one must enter into relation with the appropriate objects in the world, must work with them. Work itself is a relation between subject and object which can foreshadow the overcoming of estrangement between them, even while moving toward the realization of a utopian goal. In such ways "the world-process itself is a utopian function" (1986, 177).

Within this world-process the work of art performs a particular, and particularly important, utopian function. It is an aesthetically attempted preappearance; art for Bloch is a laboratory of forms and impulses. Of impulses, perhaps, more than forms: art is no mere blueprinting process but rather a blueprint *of* process, of that which works in the dark hollow of the Now. We recall that Bloch's favorite art is music. This is because it "provides the best access to the hermeneutics of the emotions, especially the expectant emotions" (1986, 1070) and moreover because "only music works explosively" (1986, 216). Yet all works of art worthy of the name, according to Bloch, approach this explosion, circle around this hollow space. The work is "often rounded, never closed" (1986, 217). It is not only fissured by otherness, it displays those fissures: "All great art shows the pleasant and homogeneous aspects of its work-based coherence broken, broken up, leafed open by its own iconoclasm, wherever immanence is not driven to closedness of form and content, wherever it still poses as *fragment-like*" (1986, 219).

It is time to return to the fragment from *Gravity's Rainbow*.

4

That passage, with its fragmentary headline and wirephoto of the nuclear cloud, has been analyzed by way of its genital associations, but it ends with a suggestion that the image of the Hiroshima bomb can be analyzed along quite different lines: "It is not only a sudden white genital onset in the sky—it is also, perhaps, a Tree." That tree branches in many ways. A number of its associations are commonplace, such as the link between the Tree of Eden and the Cross: Tree of Eden, sign of the fall (complete with an earlier reference to the "serpent head" of the penis that is a cannon); the Cross, sign of redemption, as crucifixion imaging bodily pain that validates an ideology, perhaps that of Caesar, perhaps that of Christ. In this way a scene of scapegoating, of sacrifice to the Father; a few lines later there is a reference to "the city about to be sacrificed." The Tree is also Yggdrasil, the World Tree of Norse mythology, on which Odin hung for three days and nights in order to earn the right to the runes of knowledge. The cloud, like the tree, will overspread the world, just as the Kabbala's Tree of Life is "the axis of a particular Earth, a new dispensation, brought into being by the Great Firing" (Pynchon 1973, 753). All these associations, and no doubt others, contribute to the Tree's iconic power—or, as Pynchon puts it, its "hey-lookit-me smugness." But beyond its branching associations the Tree may evoke the text's very ability to produce such associations, and consequently to cross over into the unconscious.

In his essay on "The Agency of the Letter in the Unconscious" Lacan contrasts two uses of the signifier "Tree": first, as the equivalent of a tree's image, which never crosses the bar between signifier and signified; second, in some lines by Valéry where it does cross the bar, exemplifying an important concept:

> There is in effect no signifying chain that does not have, as if attached to the punctuation of each of its units, a whole articulation of relevant contexts suspended 'vertically,' as it were, from that point. (Lacan 1977, 154)

Pynchon's Tree itself is only one of the relevant contexts held in suspension by his layered, highly charged language here. That these contexts are brought to the text by its acculturated reader in no way detracts from Pynchon's accomplishment, which is to make audible a certain polyphony of language beyond its "official" function. This, Lacan tells us, can be heard if one listens to language and writes accordingly:

> What this structure of the signifying chain discloses is the possibility I have, precisely in so far as I have this language in common with other subjects, that is to say, in so far as it exists as a language, to use it in order to signify *something quite other* than what it says. This function of speech . . . is no less than the function of indicating the place of [the] subject in the search for the true.
>
> I have only to plant my tree in a locution; climb the tree, even project on to it the cunning illumination a descriptive context gives to a word; raise it (*arborer*) so as not to let myself be imprisoned in some sort of *communiqué* of the facts, however official, and if I know the truth, make it heard. (1977, 155)

The official communiqué—in Pynchon the occupation newspaper—is appropriated in the interests of making heard a very different truth, something quite other, about the Other, if only at the level of the unconscious—where all discourse has its effect. And that effect may be of the future, may even effect a future.

For Lacan the function of language is "no less than the function of indicating the place of [the] subject in the search for the true." The true for Lacan is the unconscious, which manifests itself through that which is latent in language. The best language, then, would be one in which the branching associations can flourish and grow. It is significant, however, that it is a *process of growth* that is rendered. The "truth" of the unconscious is not a stable one, nor is the unconscious "as such" even attainable. Rather the language here mirrors the subject, a subject in continual motion; the function of language is not, for instance, "representation," but a more vague and ongoing "indicating." And what language is indicating, moreover, is not "the true" but the subject's *search* for the true in the unconscious. This emphasis on growth, process, search, makes Lacan's psychoanalysis more congenial to Bloch's philosophy than Bloch himself would be ready to believe. Psychoanalysis for him is backward-looking, knowledge from the back: "The unconscious of psychoanalysis is . . . never a *Not-Yet-Conscious,* an element of progressions; it consists rather of regressions" (1986, 56). But there is a sense in which for the night's dream no less than the day's "its latency lies ahead" (1986, 99). In the darkness that both the now and the unconscious share, something "ferments," in Bloch's phrase, urgently seeking the daylight. Where that force finds itself blocked it branches, ramifies, in a labyrinth so rich as to include contradictory directions, signaling wishes by denials, calling to remembrance by acts of forgetting. And when the moment in psychoanalysis is reached when one paradoxically remembers forgetting, the effect is not that of a stable goal attained; rather of a radical destabilizing, indeed an explosion of self. But this is not the terminus. The explosion may serve the same function as it does in Bloch: destruction of false or inadequate Becomeness, opening up a space for new, interminable process.

For such reasons as these, the very sliding of signs, the radical instability of language, can be a principle of hope—as is unexpectedly exemplified in the passage Lacan quotes from Valéry:

No! says the Tree, it says No! in the shower of sparks
  Of its superb head.
Which the storm treats as universally
  As it does a blade of grass.

The sparks showering from the tree indicate an explosive force; and, as in Bloch, that force is an "annihilation of inadequate becomeness." Here, perhaps, the inadequacy is that of the "classic yet faulty illustration" depicting the tree's image over the word *tree*. But this Tree says No! to that concept or official communiqué. Instead, the poetic resources of Valéry's language make manifest another kind of tree, a tree beheld in the unconscious, perhaps the tree *of* the unconscious—which is also the tree of language. The explosive force has its locus, then, not in any signified tree but in the signifiers. These signifiers, Lacan's analysis indicates, create this tree—a tree that corresponds to nothing in the already existing world. If anything, it corresponds to the continual search for the "true," whose ultimate truth may be that it is never to be realized, and never to be abandoned. The search is here indicated through the apparently imminent destruction of the stable "official" sign.

Let us set the tree's force against the explosive force of what might be called a nuclear tree, branching out in uncountable fissions to yield its barren fruit. In *Riddley Walker* nuclear power is found at the "heart of the wood." But that phrase branches out in various associations and contexts until it finally turns back upon itself, becoming the heart of the *would*, of the wanting to be. The tree of language, then, can bring forth a future—if not as fruit, at least as Bloch's "core which seeks its fruit." And this can be done in the face of that other, nuclear tree, resisting its nothingness through language's paradoxical being.

No! says the Tree, it says No! in the shower of sparks
  Of its superb head.

That No! is an affirmation, an opening into hope.

The Final Word

After the final No there comes a Yes.
  —Wallace Stevens, "The Well Dressed Man with a Beard"

There is nowhere any last word unless in the sense in which
word is *not a word.*
  —Lacan, *Feminine Sexuality*

The "last word" names the place where the "nonfirstness" of
the first word repeats itself.
  —Barbara Johnson, *The Critical Difference*

This word never begins, but always speaks anew and is always
starting over.
  —Blanchot, *The Space of Literature*

It is up to the reader to give the letter what he will find as its
last word: its destination.
  —Lacan, "Seminar on *The Purloined Letter*"

A letter can always not arrive at its destination, and . . .
therefore it never arrives.
  —Derrida, *The Post Card*

Pure Discourse: . . . the work of the "No" in its multiple forms behind which reading, and writing, prepare for the advent of a "Yes" both unique and ever reiterated in the circularity where there is no longer any first and last affirmation.

—Blanchot, *The Writing of the Disaster*

Works Cited

Auster, Paul. 1987. *In the Country of Last Things*. New York: Viking.

Bartter, Martha A. 1986. "Nuclear War as Urban Renewal." *Science Fiction Studies* 39: 148–58.

Basford, Kathleen. 1978. *The Green Man*. Ipswich: D. S. Brewer.

Bataille, Georges. 1985. *Visions of Excess: Selected Writings, 1927–1939*. Trans. A. Stoekl with C. R. Lovitt and D. M. Leslie. Minneapolis: U of Minnesota P.

Benjamin, Walter. 1968. *Illuminations*. Ed. Hannah Arendt. Trans. Harry Zohn. New York: Harcourt, Brace & World.

Bettelheim, Bruno. 1962. *Symbolic Wounds: Puberty Rites and the Envious Male*. New York: Collier.

Blanchot, Maurice. 1978. "Il n'est d'explosion . . ." in *Misère de la Litterature*. Paris: Christian Bourgois.

———. 1981. *The Gaze of Orpheus and Other Literary Essays*. Ed. P. Adams Sitney. Trans. Lydia Davis. Barrytown, N.Y.: Station Hill.

———. 1982. *The Space of Literature*. Trans. Ann Smock. Lincoln: U of Nebraska P.

———. 1986. *The Writing of the Disaster*. Trans. Ann Smock. Lincoln: U of Nebraska P.

Bloch, Ernst. 1986. *The Principle of Hope*. Trans. Neville Plaice, Stephen Plaice, and Paul Knight. Cambridge, Mass.: MIT P.

Bonaparte, Marie, Anna Freud, and Ernst Kris, eds. 1954. *The Ori-*

gins of Psychoanalysis: Letters to Wilhelm Fliess, Drafts and Notes, 1887–1902. New York: Basic Books.

Brin, David. 1986. The Postman. New York: Bantam.

Brooks, Peter. 1977. "Freud's Masterplot." Yale French Studies 55/56: 280–300.

Derrida, Jacques. 1978a. "Ellipsis" in Writing and Difference. Trans. Alan Bass. Chicago: U of Chicago P.

———. 1978b. "Structure, Sign and Play in the Discourse of the Human Sciences" in Writing and Difference. Trans. Alan Bass. Chicago: U of Chicago P.

———. 1981. Dissemination. Trans. Barbara Johnson. Chicago: U of Chicago P.

———. 1982. "Différance." In Margins of Philosophy. Trans. Alan Bass. Chicago: U of Chicago P.

———. 1984. "No Apocalypse, Not Now (full speed ahead, seven missiles, seven missives)." Diacritics 14: 20–31.

———. 1987. The Post Card: From Socrates to Freud and Beyond. Trans. Alan Bass. Chicago: U of Chicago P.

Einstein, Albert. 1975. Einstein on Peace. Ed. Otto Nathan and Heinz Norden. New York: Schocken.

Ferguson, Frances. 1984. "The Nuclear Sublime." Diacritics 14: 4–10.

Foucault, Michel. 1977. "What is an Author?" in Language, Counter-Memory, Practice. Trans. Donald F. Bouchard and Sherry Simon. Ithaca: Cornell UP.

Freeman, Barbara. 1989. "Amour postmoderne et désir nucléaire." Les Cahiers du Grif 41/42: 129–39.

Freud, Sigmund. 1965 [1900]. The Interpretation of Dreams. Trans. James Strachey. New York: Avon.

Gee, Maggie. 1983. The Burning Book. New York: St. Martin's.

Girard, René. 1977. Violence and the Sacred. Trans. Patrick Gregory. Baltimore: Johns Hopkins UP.

———. 1978. "To Double Business Bound": Essays on Literature, Mimesis and Anthropology. Baltimore: Johns Hopkins UP.

Glass, Philip. 1979. Einstein on the Beach. Tomato, TOM-4-2901.

Hachiya, Michihiko. 1955. Hiroshima Diary. Ed. Warner Wells. Chapel Hill: U of North Carolina P.

Heidegger, Martin. 1975. "The Anaximander Fragment" in *Early Greek Thinking*. Trans. D. F. Krell and F. A. Capuzzi. New York: Harper & Row.

Hoban, Russell. 1982. *Riddley Walker*. London: Picador.

Jameson, Fredric. 1981. *The Political Unconscious: Narrative as a Socially Symbolic Act*. Ithaca: Cornell UP.

Johnson, Barbara. 1981. *The Critical Difference: Essays in the Contemporary Rhetoric of Reading*. Baltimore: Johns Hopkins UP.

Johnson, Denis. 1985. *Fiskadoro*. New York: Knopf.

Kierkegaard, Søren. 1964. *Repetition: An Essay in Experimental Psychology*. Princeton: Princeton UP.

———. 1971. *Philosophical Fragments*. Trans. D. F. Swenson and H. V. Hong. Princeton: Princeton UP.

Kristeva, Julia. 1980. *Desire in Language: A Semiotic Approach to Literature and Art*. Trans. L. S. Roudiez. New York: Columbia UP.

———. 1982. *Powers of Horror: An Essay in Abjection*. Trans. L. S. Roudiez. New York: Columbia UP.

Lacan, Jacques. 1970. "Of Structure as an Inmixing of Otherness Prerequisite to Any Subject Whatever" in *The Structuralist Controversy: The Languages of Criticism and the Sciences of Man*, Richard Macksey and Eugenio Donato, eds. Baltimore: Johns Hopkins UP.

———. 1972. "Seminar on *The Purloined Letter*." *Yale French Studies* 48: 38–72.

———. 1977. *Ecrits: A Selection*. Trans. Alan Sheridan. New York: Norton.

———. 1979. *The Four Fundamental Concepts of Psycho-Analysis*. Ed. Jacques-Alain Miller. Trans. Alan Sheridan. New York: Penguin.

———. 1985. *Feminine Sexuality*. Ed. Juliet Mitchell and Jacqueline Rose. New York: Norton.

Lawrence, D. H. 1968. *Phoenix II: Uncollected, Unpublished and Other Prose Works by D. H. Lawrence*. Ed. Warren Roberts and Harry T. Moore. New York: Viking.

Leiris, Michel. 1963. *Manhood: A Journey from Childhood into the Fierce Order of Virility*. Trans. Richard Howard. New York: Grossman.

Levinas, Emmanuel. 1981. *Otherwise than Being or Beyond Essence*. Trans. A. Lingis. Boston: Martinus Nijhoff.

Lifton, Robert Jay. 1967. *Death in Life: Survivors of Hiroshima*. New York: Random House.

Lifton, Robert Jay, and Robert Falk. 1982. *Indefensible Weapons: The Political and Psychological Case against Nuclearism*. New York: Basic Books.

MacCannell, Dean. 1984. "Baltimore in the Morning . . . After: On the Forms of Post-Nuclear Leadership." *Diacritics* 14: 33–44.

MacCannell, Juliet Flower. 1986. *Figuring Lacan: Criticism and the Cultural Unconscious*. Lincoln: U of Nebraska P.

Malamud, Bernard. 1982. *God's Grace*. New York: Farrar Straus Giroux.

Maniquis, Robert. 1983. "Pascal's Bet, Totalities, and Guerilla Criticism." *Humanities in Society* 6: 133–38.

Meyers, Edward. 1984. "An Interview with Russell Hoban." *Literary Review* 28: 5–16.

O'Brien, Tim. 1985. *The Nuclear Age*. New York: Knopf.

Perlman, Michael. 1988. *Imaginal Memory and the Place of Hiroshima*. Albany: SUNY P.

Pynchon, Thomas. 1973. *Gravity's Rainbow*. New York: Viking.

Reich, Steve. 1984. *The Desert Music*. Nonesuch. 7559–79101–1.

Roth, Philip. 1974. *My Life as a Man*. New York: Holt, Rinehart & Winston.

Rotman, Brian. 1987. *Signifying Nothing: The Semiotics of Zero*. London: Macmillan.

Salusinszky, Imre, ed. 1987. *Criticism in Society*. New York: Methuen.

Scarry, Elaine. 1985. *The Body in Pain: The Making and Unmaking of the World*. New York: Oxford UP.

Schell, Jonathan. 1982. *The Fate of the Earth*. New York: Knopf.

Szilard, Leo. 1978. *Leo Szilard: His Version of the Facts: Selected Recollections and Correspondence*. Ed. Spencer R. Weart and Gertrud Weiss Szilard. Cambridge, Mass.: MIT P.

Tarkovsky, Andrey. 1986. *Sculpting in Time: Reflections on the Cinema*. London: Bodley Head.

———. 1987. *Opfer*. Munich: Schirmer/Mosel.

Taylor, Mark C. 1987. *Altarity.* Chicago: U of Chicago P.

Townsend, Peter. 1984. *The Postman of Nagasaki.* London: Collins.

Treat, John. 1989. "Hiroshima and the Place of the Narrator." *Journal of Asian Studies* 48: 29–49.

Weart, Spencer R. 1988. *Nuclear Fear: A History of Images.* Cambridge, Mass.: Harvard UP.

Winnett, Susan. 1990. "Coming Unstrung: Women, Men, Narrative, and Principles of Pleasure." *PMLA* 105: 505–18.

Wordsworth, William. 1985. *The Fourteen-Book Prelude.* Ithaca: Cornell UP.

Index